DOWNLOAD
for Parents

Sex, Social Media, and Secrets

John Sternfels, LPC

Fulton Books
Meadville, PA

Published by Fulton Books 2025

ISBN 979-8-89221-382-0 (paperback)
ISBN 979-8-89221-403-2 (hardcover)
ISBN 979-8-89221-383-7 (digital)

Printed in the United States of America

Also by John Sternfels

A Partner's Guide To Truth & Healing: A
Healing Journey For Betrayed Partners
Behind the Smile: Healing from Abuse, Trauma, and Betrayal

"There are no perfect parents, and there are no perfect children, but there are plenty of perfect moments along the way."
– Dave Willis

Contents

Introduction
Sex, Social Media, and Secrets, Oh My!

Parenting can bring immense joy and fulfillment as you witness and participate in your child's growth, development, and achievements. The boundless love you have for your child and the love they give you in return is a profound and unparalleled joy of parenting.

Whether celebrating your child's first steps, first words, academic successes, or other milestones is incredibly rewarding and brings immense fulfillment. As a father of three sons, I have found profound joy that has brought love, nurture, growth, and connection—all designed to last a lifetime.

Parenting is also a complex and demanding role that presents many challenges. Balancing work and family commitments can be a perpetual struggle, often causing stress and fatigue, as parents strive to provide both financially and emotionally for their children. Technological advancements have brought about new challenges, including navigating the digital landscape and ensuring children's safety in an online world.

Moreover, the fast-paced, competitive society places immense pressure on children, leading to academic stress and mental health issues. Influences from peers, media, and societal expectations add to the challenge of guiding children toward positive values and decisions.

Additionally, differing parenting philosophies, generational gaps, and diverse family structures require parents to adapt and find the right approach that suits their unique circumstances. Parenting demands constant learning, patience, and resilience to overcome these and numerous other obstacles in the journey of nurturing and raising children.

Times are changing as nearly half of parents today raise their children differently than how they were raised, feeling pressured to be hands-on. A recent study (2022) concluded that more than three out of five parents today need to spend more time with their children than their parents spent with them.

The survey concluded that parents spend an average of five hours daily with their children today. Parent-and-child activities include during meals (32%), watching television or movies (30%), playing (27%), getting their children ready for bedtime (27%), and for bath time (26%).

Parents today may think that one-on-one time and the availability of new technology would make parents' lives much more manageable. However, it is reported that parents "have been conditioned to find ways to involve themselves, even when kids are on task and actively playing or doing what they've been asked to do so."[1]

So what is the difference between traditional and modern parenting? Generally, traditional parenting involves stricter rules and discipline, whereas modern parenting is more "open-minded" and less rigid. Traditional parenting tends to rely on rewards and punishment while modern parenting focuses more on opportunities for "teachable moments." The focus is more on teaching life lessons through parent-and-child dialogs.

Regardless of style, parent-child interaction is vital, especially in elementary school, when children learn to manage their attention, emotions, and behaviors without their parents' help.[2] Although this may seem contrary to many parents, parents must pull back and allow their children to discover "teachable moments" independently. Sometimes, kids need to learn to be alone and allowed to discover their new world, of course, in a safe way.

---

[1] https://news.stanford.edu/2021/03/11/study-reveals-impact-much-parental-involvement/.

[2] Ibid.

As all of us know, adolescence is a critical time as children transition into becoming adults. Development factors include intellectual, physical, hormonal, and social. This time in human development is a vital period in brain maturation. Children become exceptionally vulnerable to impulse control when seeking information on social media platforms.

For clarity, social media is any online platform and application enabling users to create, share, and interact with content in a virtual social environment.[3] These platforms facilitate communication and networking, allowing individuals, organizations, and businesses to connect with others, express themselves, and share various types of content, such as text, images, videos, and links.

Sexual content is highly prevalent in our culture today. Various influences include television, music, photographs, sculptures, paintings, animations, sound recordings, films, social media, books, magazines, cartoons, posters, postcards, and video games, as well as many others.

For the purpose of this book, I will define sexual content as meaning *any material showing sexual behavior.* Sexual behavior may be implied, inferred, hinted at, suggested, or explicit, even in text.

It is important to know that the Internet has dramatically increased the ease of use in providing exposure to sexual content for anyone with just one click. It is well-documented that prolonged exposure may also lead to becoming an addiction.

An American Psychological Association (APA) research study found that

> The advent of the Internet has added another medium in which people can engage in sexual behavior. This ranges from the passive consumption of online pornography to the interactive exchange of sexual content in cybersex chat rooms. It is believed that access, affordability, and anonymity are critical factors that make

---

3   Ibid.

the Internet viable for the acquisition, development, and maintenance of online sexuality…It was concluded that engaging in sexual behaviors on the Internet can go awry and result in Internet sex addiction, as it can lead to a wide variety of negative consequences for the individuals affected.[4]

Research has also found that nearly all teens (95%) ages 13 to 17 use social media.[5] The average age of adolescents viewing pornography online is 14 for boys and 17.5 for girls.[6] It is also well-documented that about 92% of US adolescents between the ages of 13 and 17 use the Internet daily.[7]

Parents need to become more aware and involved in their children's lives by managing the use of social media. Social media use increases the risk of depression, anxiety, sleep disturbances, low self-esteem, body image confusion, eating disorders, or even online harassment or bullying.[8]

When it comes to keeping secrets, children, like adults, keep secrets for various reasons, often influenced by their developmental stage, environment, and individual personality.

---

[4] MD Griffiths, "Internet Sex Addiction: A Review of Empirical Research," 2012, https://core.ac.uk/download/30641827.pdf.

[5] "Social Media's Concerning Effect on Teen Mental Health," www.aecf.org.

[6] D. Herbenick, T. Fu, P. Wright, B. Paul, R. Gradus, J. Bauer, and R. Jones, "Diverse Sexual Behaviors and Pornography Use: Findings from a Nationally Representative Probability Survey of Americans Aged 18 to 60 Years," *The Journal of Sexual Medicine* 20 (2020): 623–633.

[7] A. Lenhart, "Teens, Social Media and Technology Overview 2015," www.pewinternet.org/2015/04/09/teens-social-media-technology-2015/.

[8] "Should You Take a Break from Social Media?" Soul Purpose, https://staceylepitre.com/should-you-take-a-break-from-social-media/.

Common reasons why children might keep secrets:

Fear of punishment.

Children may keep secrets to avoid getting into trouble or facing punishment from their parents, caregivers, or teachers. They may fear negative consequences for their actions and choose to hide certain information to protect themselves.

Desire for autonomy.

As children grow and develop, they seek a sense of independence and autonomy. Keeping secrets can be a way for them to assert their independence and control over aspects of their lives, especially if they feel that sharing certain information may lead to parental intervention or restrictions.

Protection of privacy.

Children, like anyone else, value their privacy. They may keep secrets to maintain a sense of personal boundaries and privacy, especially regarding thoughts, feelings, or experiences they are not ready for or comfortable sharing with others.

Peer pressure or social dynamics.

Children may keep secrets to fit in with their peers or avoid being ostracized or bullied. They might withhold certain information to align with the norms and expectations of their social group, even if it means keeping something hidden from adults.

Emotional reasons.

Children may keep secrets related to emotional experiences or challenges they are facing. They may struggle with difficult emotions, relationships, or experiences, and sharing these secrets might make them feel vulnerable, ashamed, or embarrassed.

Testing boundaries.

Children often test the limits of what they can get away with, and keeping secrets can be a way to push their parents' or caregivers' boundaries. They may want to see if they can keep information hidden without being discovered.

Avoidance of conflict or stress.

Children might keep secrets to avoid causing conflicts or adding stress to their families or caregivers. They may think that revealing certain information could lead to tension, arguments, or additional stress within the family.

Regardless of the reason, parents need to create a safe and open environment where children feel comfortable discussing their thoughts, feelings, and experiences.[9] Encouraging them with open communications, building trust, and understanding the reasons behind every secrecy can help foster a healthy relationship and address any concerns or issues the child might have.

---

[9] "Teaching Kids Internet Safety," Internxt Blog, https://blog.internxt.com/internet-safety-for-kids/.

Section 1
Sexual Development

*Parents are the sex educators of their children—
whether they do it well or badly.*

—Dr. Sol. Gordon

Parental downloading

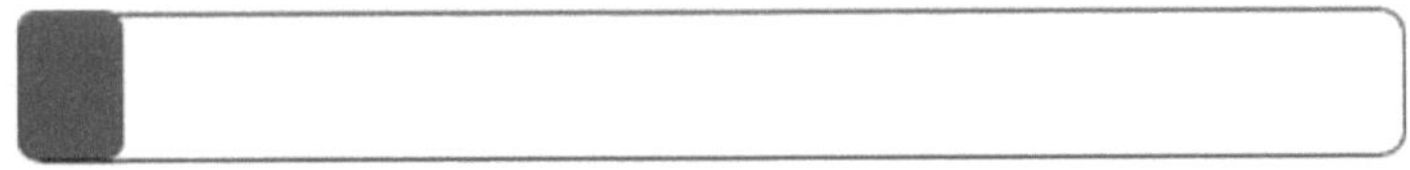

Estimated time left: 4 hours and 27 seconds

C: reader//87953:downloading_sexual_development

Chapter 1
Preschooler Sexual Development (Age 3–6)

Sexual development in children ages three to six is an important and natural part of their overall development. It's crucial to approach this topic with care and sensitivity. At this stage, children are becoming aware of their bodies and starting to form their understanding of gender and sexuality.

Parents can begin teaching their children about their body parts during bath time. Teaching can be as easy as naming a body part and then asking your child to repeat what you said. If your child points to a particular body part, be at ease and use the proper anatomical term. Note: If your child experiences your uneasiness or uncomfortableness, your child may grow to learn that asking questions about their body parts is not permissible or wrong.

When it comes to brain development, it is not the scope of this book to provide an in-depth understanding of early brain development but rather to provide a basic understanding of what influences can cause harm to the child's brain. Get some coffee or tea along with a highlighter as we learn about one particular brainwave called theta.

Children operating in the theta are very much connected to their internal world. Dr. B. Lipton, a pioneer in the field of biology, writes, "Theta is the catalyst for childhood imagination and sculpting the subconscious, which is perceived reality from age 0–7."

From birth to age six is considered the most impactful time in their life as their brains are in what is known as the theta state. Theta brain rhythm waves (3–6 hertz) are most commonly associated with social processing.[1] This is important because the child's brain is soaking everything in. The child is learning how to exist in the world. How to bond with parents. Learning about self and others. It is essential to know that everything spoken to the child gets internalized without question—including messages of who they are and others.

During this age, the child's brain records all sensory experiences, downloading massive amounts of information about themselves and the world—how it works. By observing the behavioral patterns of their parents and others, the child begins to distinguish acceptable and unacceptable behaviors. Lipton states, "It is important to realize that perceptions acquired before age six become the fundamental subconscious programs that helps shape us as individuals."[2] Furthermore, Lipton reports, "As a child, [their] perceptions of the world are directly downloaded into the subconscious during this time without discrimination and without filters of the analytical self-conscious mind which doesn't fully exist."[3]

> **"It is important to realize that perceptions acquired before age six become the fundamental subconscious programs that helps shape us as individuals."**

I realize this may be a bit of information overload. Still, it is important to understand the most significant influencer in your child's inner world. The critical takeaway is that children are influenced by the programming they receive, which would inevitably influence 95 percent of their behavior for the rest of their lives.[4] Understanding the development of the child's brain, along with helping them understand their body (i.e., sexual development), works best when started early in one's life.

Parents need to understand that children often become more aware of their bodies during this age range and may start to notice the

---

1 Bruce Lipton, PhD.
2 Ibid.
3 Ibid.
4 Ibid.

physical differences between boys and girls. It is important to note that parents should teach their children the correct anatomical terms when referring to the child's various body parts. Using slang terms may cause confusion or shame for the child. It is also understandable, as a parent, that you may feel embarrassed or uncomfortable speaking the proper anatomical term. Therefore, parents are encouraged to use the appropriate anatomical terms to make it natural and comfortable for themselves and their children as they become healthy, mature, stable adults.

As children continue to grow, they will ask questions about sex. It is natural for them and you to properly engage in healthy discussions about their curiosity regarding their bodies and sex. Having the vocabulary and ease about sex provides the child ownership of their bodies and the knowing it is okay to talk about their body parts without embarrassment or shame.

More specifically, it is around age two that children generally begin to notice physical differences between boys and girls. It is common for children to engage in playful dress-ups that are associated with the opposite sex. A boy may pretend to be like Mom, and a girl may pretend to be like Daddy. This behavior is quite typical and expected. This kind of playful dress-up does not mean the child is *gay* or something is *wrong* with them. When children continue to explore their bodies, parents may feel uncomfortable, embarrassed, or even shocked seeing them explore their bodies this way.[5]

During this phase in the child's sexual development, parents need to become comfortable discussing the "M" word. Understandably, this is a very personal and sensitive subject matter for many. Nonetheless, the subject is about masturbation.

Curiosity, exploration, and masturbation (*masturbation defined here as seeking pleasure, reward, or comfort through touching one's genitals*) are normal human behaviors during this phase of the child's human sexual development. Remember, masturbation, defined here, is the "touching" of one's genitals.

---

[5] https://www.zerotothree.org/resource/sexual-health-and-safety/.

Focus on the Family, a Christian-based organization that provides radio broadcasts, websites, simulcasts, conferences, interactive forums, magazines, books, etc. and equips parents, children, and spouses to thrive in an ever-changing, ever-more-complicated world through the various resources listed above.

When kids enter school, they become more aware of culture and others' behaviors. Beginning a conversation about masturbation tends to be more accessible. Especially when children are four to eight years old, kids are likelier to talk openly.

For school-age kids, masturbation is sometimes used as a self-soothing behavior. When kids feel lonely or rejected by classmates, doubt creeps in. When kids self-soothe in this age group, they will most likely hide their behavior from their parents or caregivers.

During this age and stage of development, knowing what to do when your kids masturbate depends on various factors. However, it is crucial to note that parents should not avoid discussing masturbation behaviors with their children.

Dr. M Systema, a licensed professional counselor, states, "If we avoid the topic, we're allowing guilt and shame to build in a child, which is more destructive than many other things in a child's life."

Those early conversations don't have to be descriptive, but they should not be so vague that their children do not know what is being discussed. Talking about masturbation *must* be in a natural (voice) tone. Explaining how certain body parts feel good when touched can help parents pave the way for open and honest conversations later.

Then, the conversation can move to the boundaries for this type of touch. "Failure to discuss openly with your child confuses them as they have no context for their feelings and what is and is not okay."

Parents should work hard to avoid condemning messages, such as looking horrified and bursting into tears or yelling *"Don't ever do that!"* Punishing a child for masturbating is another form of shaming, as is telling him that masturbation is going to ruin his future sex life, prevent him from having children, or grow hair on his palms.

While shaming may stop the behavior, it does not work effectively toward the higher goal of raising a healthy, mature, stable adult. A more beneficial response is to consider asking the child whether they are feeling lonely or afraid, as it may result from something much bigger that is going on in their life.[6]

There is a point when a child's "normal" discovery may turn into unhealthy body-pleasing behavior (i.e., masturbation), which will need to be addressed.

Common sexual soothing behaviors may include the following:

1) The child cannot stop touching their genitals, where sexual exploration may become compulsive.
2) The child attempts to involve others in the "touching" or "show me yours, and I will show you mine" activities.
3) Simulates (role-plays) adult sexual activities or uses adult sexual rhetoric (e.g., f—— k, blow jobs, etc.).
4) Begins to exhibit toilet accidents (after learning how to use the toilet), frequently bed-wetting, or increased behavioral/ emotional difficulties.

The National Center on the Sexual Behavior of Youth provides an easy understanding of essential childhood development.

Young children seek pleasure. They do not see themselves from other people's viewpoints. They are not self-conscious.

They may lack modesty and want to be comfortable. They will undress and run around nude in front of others. They may appear to not care about how other people feel because they don't fully understand the impact of their behavior on others.

They are curious about the world, how things work, and how things are similar and different from one another.

They are curious about physical differences between boys and girls and between children and adults. This curiosity includes wanting to see how boy's and girl's body parts are different.

Children learn through their senses, especially by using sight and touch.

They are acquiring a growing vast vocabulary.

---

[6] https://www.focusonthefamily.com/parenting/what-to-do-when-young-kids-masturbate/.

They use words related to urination ("pee-pee") and defecation ("poo-poo") when labeling their private parts. These words can be exciting to children who will use these words repeatedly, particularly with other kids. Young children will use the anatomical words (such as vagina, vulva, penis, anus) if taught these terms consistently.

They learn about behaviors by watching and imitating the people around them (primarily parents and other family members).

They imitate the behaviors of other children and adults and play "doctor," "house," or "mommy and daddy" with other children.

Children want to avoid being punished by their parents. They try to avoid discomfort, including getting in trouble. They want approval, praise, and rewards from their parents.

Whether or not a child repeats sexual behavior is often related to how caregivers respond to the child's initial sexual behavior.

Preschool children have limited ability to plan and control their behavior. They have a poor understanding of the long-term consequences of their behavior.

Children's typical sexual behavior (such as curiously looking at another child) is unplanned. The behavior is impulsive, without much thought.

Children often play make-believe. They often pretend to be something or someone else. They may play or dress up as people of the opposite sex.

All children need to develop a greater sense of healthy body awareness; it is crucial never to punish or shame them because they are discovering their genitals. Punishing or conveying disapproval can cause the child to feel "bad" or "dirty," resulting in developing an unhealthy sense of their sexuality.

"Sexually explicit, planned, or aggressive sexual acts are not a typical part of sexual development. Other rare unhealthy sexual behaviors include putting objects in the vagina or rectum, putting one's mouth on sexual parts, or pretending toys are having sex."[7]

---

[7]   https://www.ncsby.org/content/childhood-sexual-development.

Chapter 2
School-Age Sexual Development (Age 6–12)

Each stage of development encompasses specific markers, and as such, this stage, especially, parents will start to see a transition as they move from playing alone to developing friends and social groups. This is also a significant time when children learn how to interact and socialize with one another.

During this developmental time, children learn to interact and socialize with others, learning what is socially acceptable and what is not. Additionally, it is important to continue fostering the child's physical, emotional, spiritual, and cognitive growth, not to mention the importance of creating healthy foundations for the child's sexual development. Note: Sexual behavior depends on the child's development, social relationships, cultural background, and personal and family experience.[1]

Below are some school-age developmental markers for parents to know about their child during this time:

Physical development.[2]

It is common for children between the ages of six to eight to:

- experience slower growth of about two and a half inches and eight pounds per year

---

[1] https://raisingchildren.net.

[2] Richa Adhikari, "Three Essays on the Use of Social Media by Arts Nonprofit Organizations," (2023), https://doi.org/10.57709/35906756.

- grow longer legs relative to their total height and begin resembling adults in the proportion of legs to body
- develop less fat and grow more muscle than in earlier years
- increase in strength
- they lose their baby teeth and begin to grow adult teeth, which may appear too big for their face
- use small and large motor skills in sports and other activities

Emotional development.[3]

Children between the ages of six and eight are becoming more modest, desire more privacy, and develop relationships with people outside the family so that family and peer support can meet their emotional needs.

During this age of development, children may be less likely physically to show love (e.g., unless directed by parents to do so, giving hugs) but rather express love through sharing and talking as children may become embarrassed by physical affection.

Parents mustn't force affection.

According to the American Academy of Pediatrics Council on Child Abuse and Neglect report:

> Do not force or guilt your children to give hugs or kisses. It is okay for them to tell even grandma or grandpa that they do not want to give them a kiss or a hug goodbye. Teach your child alternate ways to show affection and respect without close physical touch (high fives, thumbs-ups, etc.) Reinforce that their body is theirs to control, a concept called body autonomy.[4]

---

[3] Ibid.
[4] https://www.advocatesforyouth.org/.

Parents need to provide emotional stability in the home. Children need love and support but sometimes may feel less willing to ask for it.

Spiritual development.

Parents need to help their children's spiritual development. Spiritual thoughts and feelings are an integral part of not only their emotional growth process but also their spiritual development.[5] Young children's early faith experiences are most likely rooted in concrete experiences of seeing, hearing, and touching.

Children during this stage of development may still believe in Santa Claus but will learn that he is a myth. Because of this, many children may find it hard to believe in Jesus. Parents need to help their children learn how to separate fact from fiction.

> **Spiritual thoughts and feelings are an integral part of not only their emotional growth process but also their spiritual development.**

Suppose parents do not regularly share and engage with their children the whats and whys of their spiritual beliefs; in that case, their children, too, may conclude that Jesus is mythical.

Parents need to help their children learn about Jesus and to "look" for him in everyday life experiences. Parents should also share their "God moments" with their children daily. Parents may not realize there are many teachable spiritual moments if they are aware of them.

My good friend Jim recently shared a spiritual teachable moment with his son, Doug, while at McDonald's.

Jim shared that he would pick his son up after school every Friday afternoon, go to McDonald's, and get a Happy Meal to catch up on his son's week.

---

[5] "Sexual Behaviors in Young Children: What's Normal, What's Not?" HealthyChildren.org., https://www.healthychildren.org/English/ages-stages/preschool/Pages/Sexual-Behaviors-Young-Children.aspx.

On this particular Friday afternoon, while eating at McDonalds, Jim noticed his son eating his french fries one fry at a time. As Jim watched his son eating his fries, Jim reached into the bag to grab one for himself. When he reached into the bag and took one out, Doug immediately put his hand on the bag and said, "Mine." Surprised and confused, Jim quickly asked his son, "Did you buy that bag of french fries, son?"

Not knowing how to answer, his son stared back at him. Jim spoke again and reminded his son, "Who bought this bag of fries?" Before his son responded, Jim said, "Dad bought you those fries.

Jim proceeded to inform his son that he could take away the bag of fries or buy more if he wanted to. Jim reminded his son of who provided what his son was eating. Being a bit more sarcastic, Jim reminded his son he could buy fifty bags of fries if he wanted to.

Jim further stated he did not need the one french fry he reached for but needed him to understand what it means to be generous. Jim furthered the discussion by reminding his son of the source of what was provided to him. Jim wanted to take a moment and teach a biblical principle on generosity—a Christlike character.

Jim told his son, "Any time you forget the source of your provisions and blessings, you will forget where it comes from." Jim told his son, "God is our source of all things, and he wants to provide for you!" Jim took the opportunity to teach his son to share with others what God provides. Jim said that this could only come from a personal relationship with Jesus.

Jim reminded his son that we need to learn to share with others with a gracious heart— not to declare personal ownership. It is all about Christian generosity.

Jim purposely took the opportunity and made it into a spiritual teachable moment. Parents can set daily or weekly devotional time with their children to discuss God. Maybe sharing Bible truths can engage the child's young heart and mind in helping their spiritual development.

Cognitive development.[6]

Children between the ages of six to eight are developing the skills needed to process more abstract concepts and complex ideas, such as where babies come from, learn the basics of pregnancy birth, along with abstract learnings, such as using humor in conversations and viewing love as an idea that is not concrete.

Cognitive insights for parents:

- Parents need to understand children will begin to spend more time with the peer group and turn to peers for information. (They need information sources outside of family, and other adults can also become important entities in their lives.)
- Parents can help their children learn to focus on the past and future events and the present.
- Parents can help develop the child's attention span by staying focused on an activity or project.
- Parents need to monitor and teach how to improve the child's self-control, conforming to adult ideas of what is "socially acceptable and proper" behavior.
- Parents can aid by recognizing appropriateness in behavior by utilizing a token reward system or with substantive praise. (Example: "Cameron, thank you for picking up your room today. That was very thoughtful and kind.")
- Parents need to help their children understand the concepts of normality/abnormality, feel concerned with being normal and curious about differences.
- Parents need to help instruct and guide their children in what is known as individuation—the ability to grow to like and be true to themselves. This includes being able to express needs effectively.

---

[6] Richa Adhikari, "Three Essays on the Use of Social Media by Arts Nonprofit Organizations," (2023), https://doi.org/10.57709/35906756.

- Parents need to understand that children need to think for themselves and develop individual opinions, especially as they read and acquire information through appropriate media.[7]

Sexual development.

Parents need to understand that children may prefer to socialize with their own gender almost exclusively and maintain a reasonably rigid separation between genders.[8] (They may tease someone who acts in a way that does not adhere to predefined gender roles.)

Parents need to recognize the social stigmas and taboos surrounding sexuality, especially if they are nervous about the subject, because their children will pick up on this, which may cause the child to be less open about asking their parents questions.

Parents need to understand more complex ideas concerning sexuality and begin to help their children understand sexual behaviors apart from the basics of making a baby.

Children may become interested in what happens sexually between mom and dad. Parents need to be ready to address questions like this as it will become more complicated as they try to understand the relationship between sex and how babies are made.

Children may develop their own understandings about how their bodies work or where babies come from. As a result, they may also turn to their friends or the Internet for answers. Parents need to be proactive and become the primary source of help for their children to learn in safe and healthy ways.

Lessons and values children learn at this age will most likely stay with them as adults. Learning early in life (age appropriate) will encourage meaningful adult relationships later in life.

---

[7]   Richa Adhikari, "Three Essays on the Use of Social Media by Arts Nonprofit Organizations," (2023), https://doi.org/10.57709/35906756.

[8]   Ibid.

Parent takeaways for this stage of development:

- Children will look to peers, media, and other sources for information about sex and sexuality.
- Parents need to understand gender role stereotypes if presented as such.
- Children may engage in same-gender sexual exploration.
- Children need to have a stronger self-concept in terms of gender and body image.

Note: Parents must help their children develop a healthy sense of self. Today's culture seems to encourage children to figure this out independently.

Raising sexually healthy children.[9]

Parents need to help their children during this stage of sexual development. Below are relevant areas of conversations parents can initiate with their children:

- Continue to provide information about sexuality, even if a child does not ask for it. Children may ask fewer questions at these ages but still have lots of curiosity and need information about sexuality.
- Explain that there are many types of families, and all styles have equal value and deserve respect (for example, single parenting, blended, fostered, and adopted).
- Provide basic information about sexuality.
- Inform children about the changes that will take place when they begin puberty. Though most six- to eight-year-old children do not experience these changes, the age at which some begin to show signs of puberty, such as pubic

---

[9] Richa Adhikari, "Three Essays on the Use of Social Media by Arts Nonprofit Organizations," (2023), https://doi.org/10.57709/35906756.

hair, breast buds, and hair under the arms, is gradually decreasing, so children need this information sooner.

Ten Tips for Initiating Conversations about Growth, Development, and Sexuality[10]

Initiating conversations about growth, development, and sexuality may be difficult for some parents because they did not grow up in an environment where the subject was discussed. Some parents may be afraid they do not know the correct answers or feel confused about the proper amount of information to offer.

To help parents, here are ten guidelines:

1. Parents should encourage nonjudgmental communication by reassuring their children that they can talk to them about anything.
2. Parents should take advantage of teachable moments. A friend's pregnancy, a news article that peeks the child's interest, or what was found or watched online or on television—all provide an opportunity to start a conversation.
3. Parents can listen more than talk. Think about what your child is asking you. Confirm with your child that what you heard is what they meant to ask.
4. Parents can be careful not to jump to conclusions. The fact that your child asks about sex does not mean they are having or thinking about having sex.
5. Parents can answer questions simply and directly. Give factual, honest, short, and simple answers.

---

[10] Ibid.

6. Parents can respect their children's views (with discretion and discernment). Please share your thoughts and values and help your child express theirs.
7. Parents can reassure their children that they are normal—as are their questions and thoughts.
8. Parents can be sensitive as their child develops. Continue to teach them ways to make healthy decisions about sex and instruct them on how to get out of risky situations should they arise.

Note: Parents must never forget to be a safe place for their children to ask questions. Please, no blaming, shaming, or condemning!

9. Parents need to admit when they do not know the answer to a question. Parents can suggest that both can find the answer in the Bible, online, or in a library.
10. Parents need to understand that, at times, children may feel more comfortable talking with someone other than them. Together, think of other trusted adults with whom they can speak if preferred.

Chapter 3
Teen Sexual Development
(Age 13–19)

Sexual growth and development are continuous although these changes occur differently in males than females. This is a period of transition during which the teenager undergoes physical, hormonal, and psychological changes.

During this developmental age, sexual development should be understood more than biological changes. Sexual development awareness and readiness need to be much more comprehensive.

This is a time of changing emotions, urges, feelings, motivation, moral development, forms of attention, and aspects of self, including self-image, self-esteem, self-confidence, self-definition, social interactions, interpersonal interactions, and autonomy. "There are no generally achieved biological or psychological milestones during the teen years and no scientific or psychological evidence that differentiates a state of maturity as teenagers progress through development into their 20s."[1]

In other words, teens lack the cognitive and emotional development required to make healthy, intelligent sexual decisions.

During this stage of development, teens will most likely experiment sexually without having the necessary ability to cope with the consequences of their sexual interactions.

---

[1] Hegde, Anupama, Suhas Chandran, and Jigyansa I. Pattnaik, "Understanding Adolescent Sexuality: A Developmental Perspective," *Journal of Psychosexual Health* (2022), Accessed November 2, 2023, https://doi.org/10.1177/26318318221107598.

Sexual education is more critical today than prior generations, as teens are becoming more sexually active than before.[2]

A 2022 study from the Journal of Psychosexual Health entitled *Understanding Adolescent Sexuality: A Developmental Perspective* reports,

> Despite historical shifts in perceptions of gender roles and expectations, recent research suggests that men and women have different sexual ideals. This hypocritical standard dictates strict expression and experiential norms for women, whereas men are given more freedom in exploring their sexuality in adolescence. Also, the discouragement from peers to have sex is seen highly in females, whereas males face peer pressure to carry out sexual behaviors earlier than females. Gender differences have been seen in the emotions linked with sexual engagement. Boys reported feeling more proud after sex, while female said they felt "dirty" and ashamed. The sexual double standard in the perception of virginity is also highlighted, with women viewing their virginity as a gift to give to a cherished spouse, while more males saw it as a stigma and a lack of sexual opportunities.[3]

Recent research suggests that men and women have different sexual ideals.

---

[2] Ibid.

[3] Ibid.

Although physical changes start early during this phase of teen development, cognitive and emotional development also occurs along with the development of abstract thinking and reasoning.[4]

Emotionally, teens are developing a sense of identity, increasing their social involvement, increasing peer interactions, and developing sexual interests.

Males are experiencing enlargement of their genitals, the appearance of beard and mustache hairs, and their physique takes on a typical masculine shape.

Females are developing breasts; menstruation starts; their genitalia takes an adult shape; and their physique changes to a feminine type.

Behavioral experimentation such as pushing boundaries, developing autonomy, talking back, and being defiant or aggressive may increase isolating behaviors from their parents. This is a time of independence and identity development.

Teens are also naturally prone to engage in high-risk behaviors without having sufficient filters to evaluate the severe consequences (e.g., alcohol, drug, sex, pornography use) of their behavior choices.

Many teenagers often exhibit a sense of invincibility. This perception is commonly associated with adolescence and is linked to various factors, including brain development, hormones, and psychological processes.

The adolescent brain is still maturing, particularly the prefrontal cortex, which is responsible for decision-making and impulse control. This means that teenagers may not always accurately assess risks and consequences, leading to a feeling of invulnerability.

Hormonal changes during puberty can significantly influence behavior and emotions (ask any parent who has raised a teenager). Teens may feel more confident and adventurous, which can contribute to a sense of invincibility.

---

[4] Kar, K. Sujita, Ananya Choudhury, and Abhishek P. Singh, "Understanding Normal Development of Adolescent Sexuality: A Bumpy Ride," *Journal of Human Reproductive Sciences 8*, no. 2 (2015): 70–74, Accessed November 2, 2023, https://doi.org/10.4103/0974-1208.158594.

Teens lack life experiences and often feel "they know it all." Parents need to help their teens understand the potential dangers of certain activities they may engage in. A familiar faulty belief is that although they may not have encountered severe consequences for a particular behavior, this can result in the teen believing that nothing bad will happen to them.

Peer influence is always a growing concern. Teenagers are highly influenced by their peers. When their friends engage in risky behaviors or display a sense of invincibility, it can reinforce this belief.

Media and popular culture can influence faulty beliefs. Media portrayals of invincible or daring young characters can also shape teenagers' perceptions of themselves and their capabilities.

Parents, caregivers, and educators must acknowledge and understand this sense of invincibility in teenagers. Open communication, setting boundaries, and providing guidance on responsible decision-making and risk assessment can help adolescents make safer choices and navigate this challenging phase of life.

The following is a summary list of challenges teens will likely face during this development time. Start preparing your teen for this crucial phase if you haven't already. Remember, the next stage is young adult and adulthood. Parenting during these last two phases of your child's life is parentally limited. Make sure time does not slip away from you and your precious teen.

Teens and addiction.

Teens are at significant risk for developing an addiction. The Arrow House, a treatment center specializing in teen issues, writes, "Teens are more at risk for addiction than adults due to a combination of factors related to brain development, social influences, and emotional regulation."[5]

---

[5] "Adolescent Substance Abuse and the Developing Brain," https://thearrowhouse. com/substance-abuse/adolescent-substance-abuse-and-the-developing-brain/.

Common reasons why teens are more vulnerable to addiction:

Regarding brain development, the adolescent brain is still developing significantly, especially in the prefrontal cortex, which is responsible for executive functions such as decision-making, impulse control, and risk assessment. The incomplete maturation of the prefrontal cortex can lead to increased impulsivity and poor judgment in teens, making them more likely to engage in risky behaviors, including substance use.[6]

The brain's sensitivity to its rewards, neurocircuitry. The limbic system, responsible for processing emotions and rewards, is highly active during adolescence. As a result, teens are more sensitive to the rewarding effects of drugs, alcohol, nicotine, and sex, "which can contribute to the development of addiction. This heightened sensitivity to rewards can also increase risk-taking and novelty-seeking behaviors."[7]

The pressures of teen peers and social influences are heavy challenges. Negative peer pressure can lead teenagers to experiment with or engage in substance abuse. Friends or acquaintances who use drugs or alcohol may encourage their peers to do the same. The desire to fit in and be accepted can make it difficult for some teenagers to resist this pressure.

Teens tend to form social circles with like-minded individuals. Suppose a teen's peer group is involved in substance abuse; in that case, it can normalize such behavior and make it more likely that they will also participate.

Additionally, peers can provide access to drugs or alcohol. If a teenager's friends have easy access to these substances, they may become a source for obtaining them reasonably easily.

The effects of emotional regulation and stressors are also common during this stage of development. Some teens turn to substance abuse as a way to cope with stress, peer conflicts, or emotional chal-

---

[6] "Adolescent Substance Abuse and the Developing Brain," https://thearrowhouse.com/substance-abuse/adolescent-substance-abuse-and-the-developing-brain/.

[7] Ibid.

lenges. Suppose peers in their social circle use substances as a coping mechanism. In that case, it may encourage the struggling teenager to do the same. As a result, this can often create a shared camaraderie among themselves. This shared experience can make it challenging for most teenagers to distance themselves from the group.

Social influences can significantly affect how teens cope with stress and emotional challenges. Suppose substance use is the norm in their social group as a way to manage stress or emotions, in that case, they may be more likely to turn to substances as a coping mechanism.

Social occasions, such as parties, concerts, or gatherings, often involve alcohol or drug use. These events can create an environment where substance use is not only accepted but expected, making it easier for individuals to develop a habit of using substances.

When making healthy decisions, many teens struggle as they may not always fully comprehend the long-term consequences of their actions and decisions. Still, many of the choices they make during adolescence can have significant and lasting impacts on various aspects of their lives. They may also underestimate their susceptibility to addiction, leading to a false sense of security and an increased likelihood of engaging in substance use.[8]

Teenage neurodevelopment plays a crucial role in the vulnerability to addiction and the consequences of substance abuse. Adolescence is a period of significant brain development, and the ongoing maturation of the brain has both positive and negative implications for addiction.

Summary in teen development

- *Mental health concern.* Around 20 percent of teenagers experience mental health challenges, and suicide is the second leading cause of death.[9]

---

[8] "Adolescent Substance Abuse and the Developing Brain," https://thearrowhouse. com/substance-abuse/adolescent-substance-abuse-and-the-developing-brain/.

[9] https://www.apa.org/monitor/2023/07/psychologists-preventing-teen-suicide.

Teens with preexisting mental health issues are at a higher risk of developing addiction, and the co-occurrence of mental health disorders and substance abuse is a significant concern in this age group. Several factors contribute to the relationship between preexisting mental health issues and addiction. Increased vulnerability, impulsivity, co-occurring disorders, and lack of coping skills may turn to substances (or process addictions) as a maladaptive coping mechanism.

- *Peer pressure.* Teens may succumb to peer pressure more readily because they are eager to fit in and be accepted by their peers. Their lack of experience handling social pressures can make them more susceptible to poor choices. Parents must help their teens make independent, "healthy" choices while respecting their social interaction needs.
- *Communication issues.* Teens often become more independent and may withdraw from their parents. Communication can become strained, with teens expressing themselves differently. Parents should strive to maintain open, nonjudgmental communication and be good listeners.
- *Rebellion.* It's normal for teenagers to seek autonomy and challenge authority. This can manifest as defiance or rebellious behavior. Parents need to set clear boundaries and consequences while allowing for some degree of independence.
- *Academic pressure.* Many teens face academic pressures, including homework, exams, and college preparations. Parents can help by providing support and guidance without adding excessive pressure.
- *Technology and screen time.* Managing screen time and technology use can be challenging. Parents must set limits, monitor online activities, and encourage a healthy balance between technology use (screen time) and other activities.
- *Substance use and risky behaviors.* Adolescents may experiment with alcohol and drugs or engage in risky behaviors. Parents should be aware of warning signs, educate their

teens about the dangers, and provide a safe and nonjudgmental space for discussions.

- *Mood swings and emotional turmoil.* Hormonal changes during adolescence can lead to mood swings and emotional turbulence. Parents should be supportive and understanding during these times.
- *Body image and self-esteem.* Many teenagers struggle with body image and self-esteem issues. Parents can help by promoting a healthy body image and self-confidence and providing support and validation.[10]
- *Peer conflicts and bullying.* Adolescents may experience conflicts or bullying at school or online. Parents should teach conflict resolution skills and provide emotional support.
- Identity and career exploration. Teens are forming their identities and exploring potential career paths. Parents can assist by providing guidance and exposure to different experiences.
- Sexuality and relationships. Adolescents may begin to explore their sexuality and start dating. Parents should have open and honest conversations about sex, consent, and healthy relationships.
- Time management. Teens may struggle with time management skills, which can affect their academic and extracurricular activities. Parents can help by teaching time management techniques.

It's essential for parents to be understanding, patient, and empathetic while navigating these challenges with their teenagers. Establishing a strong foundation of trust and communication can make it easier to address and overcome these challenges together.

Seeking support from professionals or support groups can also be beneficial when facing challenging situations.

---

[10] "The Effects of Social Media on Children and Teenagers," updatesports.info, https://huay-online.com/the-effects-of-social-media-on-children-and-teenagers/.

Section 2
Influence of Social Media

Social media is changing the way we communicate and the way we are perceived, both positively and negatively. Every time you post a photo, or update your status, you are contributing to your own footprint and personal brand.

—Amy Jo Martin

Parental downloading

Estimated time left: 3 hours and 5 seconds

C: reader//87953:downloading_influence_of_social_media

Chapter 4
Positive and Negative Aspects of Social Media

The ever-growing emergence of social media brings significant changes to how people interact, share information, and communicate.

Social media is about information, conversation, and connection. Social media fosters interaction with others to create, share, and exchange information in virtual communities and networks.[1]

Whether for seeking information, *blogging* (i.e., casual dialog and discussion on specific topics) and *microblogging* (i.e., Twitter—now X—designed for groups or individuals to stay connected through threads of short messages), creating *social networks* for connection (i.e., Facebook), *building relationships* (i.e., LinkedIn), *broadcasting a channel* (i.e., podcasts), *marketing and sales, sharing pictures or videos* (i.e., Instagram), social media can be a fantastic resource for learning, entertainment, and connection.

A recent article entitled "Internet Safety for Kids" speaks about the ever-changing landscape of the Internet, which unfortunately increases significant risks for parents and their children.

The Internet is a vast and constantly evolving landscape filled with beautifully written content and seedy chat rooms. With all the variety of stuff that's ended up online, it can be difficult for parents to keep up with the latest trends and dangers.[2]

It is reported that children today spend an average of seven hours per day on entertainment, including watching television, using

---

[1] https://communications.tufts.edu/marketing-and-branding/social-media-overview/.

[2] https://blog.internxt.com/internet-safety-for-kids/.

cell phones, and spending time on computers and other electronic devices.[3]

Nearly 4.8 million people worldwide access social media. Reports indicate that between April 2022 and April 2023, there was a 3.2% increase year over year.

Statistically, this represents almost 60% of the global population and nearly 93% of all Internet users.[4] Breaking this down, it equals approximately 410,000 new social media users daily and 4.7 every second. Indeed, there is no denying that social media has become integral to our everyday lives.[5]

Positive Aspects of Social Media—Sexual and Nonsexual

Sexual education.

Regarding the positive aspects, sexual education on some social media platforms provides a space for sex educators, counselors, and organizations to share accurate and helpful information about sexual health, relationships, consent, and safe sex practices.[6]

Mental health.

Although social media has become an integral part of our modern life, its impact on mental health is a subject of ongoing research and debate.[7]

---

[3] "Screen Time for Kids: How Much Is Too Much?" Dignity Health, https://www.dignityhealth.org/articles/screen-time-for-kids-how-much-is-too-much.

[4] https://www.searchenginejournal.com/social-media-statistics/480507/#:~:text=Social%20Media%20Statistics%20Worldwide,increase%20year%2Dover%2Dyear.

[5] Ibid.

[6] ChatGPT, prompt "benefits of social media," October 20, 2023, OpenAI, https://chat.openai.com.

[7] Ibid.

Support and awareness.

Social media can be a source of support for individuals dealing with mental health issues. Online communities, forums, and groups provide a space for sharing experiences and seeking peer advice.[8]

"People experiencing mental illness may use social media to cope with stress and gain social resources unavailable in person."[9]

Access to information.

Social media can serve as a valuable source of information about mental health, self-care, and available resources. This can empower individuals to seek help and make informed decisions.

Social connection.

Social media can provide an environment/platform for keeping in touch with friends and family, especially for those who may be geographically distant. This promotes a sense of belonging and reduces feelings of loneliness.

Accessing positive content.

Many individuals and organizations use social media to share inspirational and uplifting content, boosting mood and providing motivation.

Expression and advocacy.

Social media allows individuals to express themselves, raise awareness about mental health issues, and advocate for changes in societal attitudes and policies related to mental health.

---

[8] Ibid.

[9] https://www.communitypsychology.com/

Social media has played a crucial role in raising awareness about issues like sexual harassment and gender equality. It serves as a platform for advocacy, organizing and promoting discussions.

Support communities.

Social media can be a valuable resource for individuals seeking support, advice, or connection with others who share similar experiences or concerns related to sexuality, sexual orientation, or challenges with gender identity.

Dating apps.

Many dating apps and websites use social media features, allowing users to connect with potential partners, share experiences, and create healthy, meaningful relationships.

Social media has become a platform for discussing sexuality, relationships, and sexual health. Disclaimer: It still poses several challenges and risks related to explicit content, privacy, and online safety.

Negative Aspects of Social Media—Nonsexual and Sexual

In a recent 2022 PEW research study, it was found that US teens (32%) who access social media say it had a negative impact on their age group. Still, only 9% believed this applied to themselves. Adding that "about half of teens say it would be difficult for them to give up social media."[10]

Regarding parents and teens, a study found that teens believe their parents have varying concerns. Here is the breakdown of what the study found. Around 22% of teens think their parents are "extremely" or "very worried." Whereas 41% believe their parents are either "not at all worried" (16%) or a "little worried" (25%) about their use of social media. And about a quarter of teens (27%) fell in

____

[10] https://www.communitypsychology.com/.

the middle, believing their parents were "somewhat worried," leaving about 9% "not sure due to not answering."[11]

It's a bit alarming indeed. As such, parents and educators must teach children and teenagers about responsible and safe social media use.

What used to be confined to print media, television, and movies, children today are exposed to messages from social media "influencers."

Social media influencers embed messages hidden in ads and video games and engage their followers (social media users) to influence power over them for commercial value.

Another 2022 study reports

> Social media users are prone to develop problematic behaviors such as excessive and addictive social media use (Turel and Qahri-saremi 2016), and this can be fostered by various social pressures (Osatuyi and Turel 2019), including presumably by social media influencers. In order to enhance their commercial success, social media influencers try to increase their followers' engagement by posting frequently and encouraging their followers to participate on their social media pages. This can motivate ongoing compulsive reward seeking by users, diminished reward sensation (tolerance), and reduced ability to control the behavior (Turel and Bechara 2021), which can underlie problematic behaviors such as addictive engagement among followers.[12]

---

[11] https://www.pewresearch.org/short-reads/2023/04/24/teens-and-social-media-key-findings-from-pew-research-center-surveys/.

[12] Farivar, Samira, Fang Wang, and Ofir Turel, "Followers' Problematic Engagement with Influencers on Social Media: An Attachment Theory Perspective," *Computers*

It is essential to recognize that the impact of social media on mental health is complex and multifaceted.[13] The effects can vary depending on factors such as individual personality, usage patterns, and the content consumed.

To maintain a healthy relationship with social media, individuals should consider moderating their use, curating their online experience, and seeking help when needed.[14]

Below are some examples of the many dangers of using social media. Parents are encouraged, age-appropriate, to regularly discuss and review the areas listed below with their children:

Autonomous Sensory Meridian Response (ASMR).

ASMR is a tingling, static-like, or goosebumps sensation responding to specific triggering due to audio or visual stimuli. These sensations are experienced from across the skull, down the back of the neck, or, for some, down the spine or limbs.[15]

When experiencing ASMR sensations, some people feel relaxed, calm, sleepy, or have an overall sense of well-being.[16]

It is worth mentioning that videos may prompt an ASMR response in its viewer, partly because ASMR can occur without the sensation of physical touch and instead through visual and auditory triggers that stimulate tactile sensations.[17]

When it comes to children and ASMR, there are a few things parents need to consider: Parents and caregivers should be mindful of the ASMR content their children are exposed to. Some ASMR videos

---

in Human Behavior 133 (2022): 107288, Accessed October 20, 2023, https://doi.org/10.1016/j.chb.2022.107288.

[13] "What Is the Impact of Social Media on Mental Health?" Rexdlcom.org., https://rexdlcom.org/what-is-the-impact-of-social-media-on-mental-health/.

[14] "Tips on How to Maintain a Healthy Relationship with Social Media," https://debut.careers/healthy-relationship-with-social-media/.

[15] https://www.nebraskamed.com/.

[16] Ibid.

[17] Ibid.

may contain explicit or inappropriate content, so curating the videos your child watches is essential to ensure they are age-appropriate.

Some parents find that ASMR can be a helpful tool to help calm and soothe children, especially those who have trouble falling asleep or dealing with anxiety. However, the effectiveness of ASMR for children varies from individual to individual.

While ASMR can be relaxing for many individuals, it may not have the same effect on all children. Some children may not experience ASMR sensations or they may not find the content appealing. It is essential to monitor your child's reaction and ensure they are comfortable with the ASMR content.

As with any digital media, it's essential to monitor your child's screen time and ensure they are not spending excessive hours watching ASMR videos. Encourage a healthy balance of screen time with other activities, such as outdoor play, reading, and family interactions.

Like many things on the Internet, there may be some individuals who create and share ASMR content with sexual undertones or explicit content. Such content is not representative of the broader ASMR community, and it can be inappropriate and potentially harmful, especially for minors.

In summary, ASMR can be a harmless and relaxing experience for some children. Still, it's essential for parents and caregivers to be mindful of the content their children are exposed to and to ensure it is age-appropriate.

Parents need open and honest communication with their children about their interests and online activities. Ask them about their ASMR preferences and make sure they feel comfortable discussing what they watch.

ASMR...can be inappropriate and potentially harmful, especially for minors.

Regarding other online platforms, three popular social media sites may raise concerns for parents. The three are Snapchat, YouTube Kids, and Reddit.

Snapchat and other programs such as YouTube Kids and YouTube Shorts are the new quick exposures to thoughts and expressions on social media. Artificial Intelligence (AI) has created some of it through YouTube Creators.

Recently, Snapchat displayed a middle-school girl's face that was AI-generated over a pornographic picture and was circulated on Snapchat without her knowledge or consent. The event occurred recently as a revenge tactic and was brought to the school's attention.

The parents were obviously concerned and upset because it cannot be taken back once something is out there. Snapchat is good at showing a snap, and then the author can have it erased after viewing it. To make matters worse, screenshots could have been taken and saved on any personal device without recourse.

YouTube Kids is a platform designed specifically for children, offering a more curated and child-friendly experience compared to the main YouTube platform.

It is well-known that YouTube Kids "has emerged as an alternative to traditional children's TV, and a plethora of popular children's videos can be found on the platform."

As such, "YouTube channels feature content popular among children of very young age. Hundreds of toddler-oriented channels on YouTube offer inoffensive, well-produced, and educational videos."[18]

It is important to note that YouTube Kids is unsuited to filter out suggestive material. Parents may believe that it does, but it does not. The concern is that children may be presented with narratives generated on YouTube Kids that may not reflect the family's beliefs.

Regarding Reddit (subreddits or threads), IP proxy and VPNs can allow children to access information from anywhere in the world. These are just a few ways for children to circumvent parental and, sometimes, school controls.

---

[18] https://encase.socialcomputing.eu/wp-content/uploads/2019/01/DisturbedYouTubeforKids.pdf.

Listed below are some concerns and challenges associated with YouTube Kids:

While YouTube Kids is intended to be a safe environment for children, some inappropriate or disturbing content can still slip through the filters and algorithms. The platform relies on automated content filtering and human moderation, which may not catch all potentially harmful or unsuitable videos.

YouTube Kids includes ads, which can sometimes be misleading or unsuitable for children. Although there are content guidelines for ads, there have been instances where inappropriate ads have been displayed to young viewers.

Concerns have been raised about the data collected from children using YouTube Kids. The platform does collect data for personalization and advertising purposes, which raises privacy concerns. In some cases, this has led to regulatory scrutiny and fines.

While educational content is available on YouTube Kids, it may not always be of high quality or accurate. Parents and guardians should review and select content carefully to ensure it aligns with their child's learning objectives.

As with any online platform, there is a risk of excessive screen time and potential addiction when children spend too much time, for example, accessing YouTube Kids. Parents should monitor their child's usage and set appropriate time limits.

Although YouTube Kids offers some parental controls and filtering options, they may not be comprehensive enough for some parents' preferences. Parents need to understand and utilize these controls effectively.

Some content creators may create content for YouTube Kids with the intent to exploit the platform's younger audience or produce content that is not genuinely educational or appropriate for children.

To address these concerns, parents and guardians can actively monitor and guide their child's use of YouTube Kids. This includes setting up parental controls, discussing safe and responsible online behavior, and actively curating content to ensure a safe and educational experience.

Android users. The Android platform emails the child once they turn thirteen, asking if they would like parental controls (built into Android) removed without the parent's knowledge.

Privacy concerns. Social media platforms often collect and share users' personal data. This can lead to privacy breaches and potentially expose sensitive information to malicious predators.

Cyberbullying. Cyberbullying is a prevalent issue on social media. Users, especially young people, may experience harassment, threats, or humiliation online, leading to emotional distress and mental health issues.

Mental health impact. Excessive use of social media has been linked to mental health problems, including anxiety, depression, and loneliness. The constant comparison to others and the pressure to curate a perfect online persona can contribute to these issues.

A recent study in 2022 confirmed that "the impact of social media… had a negative effect on student mental health."[19]

Furthermore, the same study found that "it also increased the likelihood with which students reported experiencing impairments to academic performance due to poor mental health. Additional evidence…suggests the results are due to…fostering unfavorable social comparisons."[20]

Addiction. Social media can be addictive, and excessive use can lead to decreased productivity and reduced time for real-life social interactions.[21] This can interfere with daily life responsibilities.

---

[19] "Tips on How to Maintain a Healthy Relationship with Social Media," https://debut.careers/healthy-relationship-with-social-media/.

[20] Braghieri, Luca, Ro'ee Levy, and Alexey Makarin, "Social Media and Mental Health," *American Economic Review* 11, 112 (2022): 3660–93.

[21] "Navigating Social Media for Mental Health: Tips and Strategies for a Healthy Experience," https://www.droidmodders.com/navigating-social-media-for-mental-health-tips-and-strategies-for-a-healthy-experience/.

Misinformation. Social media can be a breeding ground for the spread of misinformation and fake news. False or misleading information can have serious consequences,[22] especially concerning public health, political matters, sexual norms, and the promotion of the idea that everything is relative; there are "no truths"—everything is relative.

Cybersecurity threats. Users are vulnerable to phishing, hacking, and other cybersecurity threats on social media platforms. Sharing personal information or clicking on malicious links can lead to identity theft or other forms of cybercrime.[23]

Online sexual predators. Children and teenagers may be at risk of encountering online predators. Predators can use social media to establish contact with young users, putting them in potentially dangerous situations.

Digital footprints. Information and content shared on social media can have a long-lasting impact. Inappropriate posts, photos, or comments can affect a person's future reputation or job opportunities.

Filter bubbles and echo chambers. Social media algorithms often show users content aligning with their personal beliefs and opinions. This can lead to a reinforcement of existing biases, which limits exposure to diverse perspectives.[24]

---

[22] "The Ethics of Social Media: Navigating the Complexities of Online Interaction," Kiwibox.org, https://kiwibox.org/the-ethics-of-social-media-navigating-the-complexities-of-online-interaction/.

[23] Citation audit, https://www.seniorhelpers.com/ca/fresno/resources/blogs/2023-04-16/.

[24] "The Impact of Social Media Algorithms on Political Polarization and Democracy," Best Funny Vibrator Reviews, https://best-vibrator-review.com/2023/03/01/the-impact-of-social-media-algorithms-on-political-polarization-and-democracy/.

Time wasted. Excessive use of social media often wastes significant time on trivial activities, which could be better spent on productive or meaningful pursuits.

Physical health concerns. Prolonged use of social media, especially on smartphones, can contribute to physical health problems, including eye strain, disrupted sleep patterns, and poor posture.

Explicit sexual content. Inappropriate or explicit sexual content can be easily shared on social media platforms, often without age restrictions or appropriate content filters. This can expose minors to explicit materials or lead to unwanted online encounters, including rape, violence, and even death.

Harassment. Social media can be a breeding ground for online harassment, including sexually explicit threats, nonconsensual sharing of intimate images (often referred to as "revenge porn"), and other forms of abuse.[25]

Privacy risks. Sharing personal or intimate information about one's sex life or relationships on social media can have significant privacy risks. Data breaches, stalking, and the potential for unintended exposure are real concerns.

Sexting. Some individuals, especially teenagers, engage in sexting, which involves sending explicit photos or messages. This can lead to privacy breaches and legal consequences if shared without consent.

Addictive. Social media use can become addictive. The constant availability of sexual content on social media can lead to addiction or compulsive behavior. This can negatively impact relationships, productivity, and mental health.

---

[25] *News. Views. Hughes,* Retrieved on December 8, 2021, 7:30 a.m.–8:00 a.m. EST, from Internet Archive, https://ia-petabox.archive.org/details/ RT_20211208_123000_News._Views._Hughes/start/89/end/149?q=u.+k.+r.

Objectification and sexual objectification. Social media can contribute to the objectification of individuals, particularly women, by promoting unrealistic beauty standards and encouraging a culture of likes, followers, and superficial judgments based on appearance. It is also a breeding ground for female/ male image masturbation.

Online predators. Sexual predators may use social media platforms to target and groom potential victims, especially vulnerable individuals, including children and teenagers.

To help navigate the intersection of sex and social media safely and responsibly, individuals should be cautious about the content they share, maintain privacy settings, and practice consent and respect when engaging in sexual discussions or sharing intimate content.

Parents and guardians should educate their children about the potential risks and monitor their online activities daily, especially regarding explicit content or online relationships.

Section 3
Secrets, Fears, and Pornography

*At its core, pornography separates and severs the intended
use and beauty of God's intent for human sexuality and
turns it into an immoral and deviant commodity.*
—Paul Batura

Parental downloading

Estimated time left: 2 hour and 4 seconds

C: reader//87953:downloading_secrets_
fears_and_pornography

Chapter 5
Keeping Secrets

Our youth is a time filled with experiences, adventures, and decisions that often shape our lives. But what happens when those memories and secrets from our past remain buried, hidden, and boxed away?

Secrets from our past can be like heavy stones, weighing us down and affecting our mental and emotional health. These secrets may encompass a wide range of experiences, from childhood traumas to personal mistakes, hidden relationships, or undisclosed feelings. The act of concealing them can be both exhausting and damaging.

As we grow older, our minds tend to filter, edit, or even suppress specific memories from our youth. These could be memories of intense joy, embarrassment, heartbreak, or even trauma. Some secrets may have been pushed deep into the recesses of our minds and only resurface when triggered by specific events or circumstances.

Unearthing hidden secrets from our youth can profoundly impact our present life. It can bring closure, healing, and a better understanding of why you may react to certain situations in specific ways. It can also help you break free from patterns or habits that no longer serve you.

Discovering hidden secrets from your youth can be a challenging but rewarding journey. It may involve introspection, therapy, or even talking with those who shared those experiences with you.

A family impact letter holds significant value in various ways regarding addressing sensitive issues and fostering healthier family dynamics. A family impact letter provides a structured and thoughtful means of communication within the family. It encourages open and honest dialogue about challenging topics, breaking down the walls of silence and denial that often surround issues like trauma and addiction.

It allows each family member to express their thoughts, emotions, and concerns in a safe and nonconfrontational manner. It can be a therapeutic outlet for sharing feelings that might be difficult to express face-to-face.

By sharing your personal experiences, family members can better understand your experience, perspectives, and the pain or struggles you have endured. This can build empathy and compassion among family members.

In the context of addiction, a family impact letter can help define boundaries, expectations, and consequences for unhealthy behaviors. This clarifies the family's stance on enabling or supporting destructive habits.

A family impact letter can catalyze change, inspiring family members to take action, whether seeking therapy, attending support groups, or undergoing addiction treatment. It encourages a proactive approach to address family issues.

Ultimately, a family impact letter fosters a sense of unity and mutual support. It reminds everyone they are not alone in their struggles and reinforces the idea that the family is a source of strength and healing.

In summary, a family impact letter is a powerful tool for addressing difficult family issues, initiating change, promoting empathy, and creating a framework for healing and recovery. It underscores the importance of open communication, understanding, and unity within the family unit, paving the way for a healthier and more supportive family environment.

Note: It is important to remember that every family dynamic is unique, and what works for one situation may not apply to another. Deciding whether to reveal a secret to your family is a personal choice, and it should align with your values and what you believe is in the best interests of all parties involved. Seek support and guidance from trusted friends, professionals, or support groups to help you make the right decisions for your situation.

In the following letter, all names and identifying details of individuals have been altered to safeguard their privacy and protect their identities.

While actual events and people inspire the story within, the characters are fictionalized representations created for this narrative.

The author respects the privacy of the person's experiences, which have contributed to the content of this work, and has ensured that no harm is done to their reputation or well-being.

Any resemblance to actual individuals, living or deceased, is purely coincidental.

Below is a true story of a client who lived with hidden secrets from childhood. He began his recovery from pornography addiction with me a few years ago.

Mark has been married for fourteen years to his wife, Patty. Mark and Patty have two young children, ages ten and eight. Because it was important for Mark to be open and truthful, he decided it was best to read his family impact letter to his family during one of his sessions (Patty was present).

Dear family,

I asked you to be here today to be part of my family impact letter. My family impact letter is designed to let you get to know the real me and to rid myself of the masks I used to keep you from seeing and knowing the real me.

My letter is written in four parts. The first part is sharing a few critical moments I experienced in my childhood. I believe these experiences were incredibly impactful and challenging for me to understand at the time. The second part is to share some of the choices I made in life that were unhealthy and ultimately resulted in me developing an addiction, which I will further explain in the letter. Thirdly, I would like to share the impact of my addiction and the harm I have caused to everyone, especially my wife, Patty. In closing, I will end my letter by discussing the key lessons I have had to learn along my recovery journey.

I want to share that this letter allows me to pass on some life experiences to you and the generations to come. I want to address that within our family, there have been addictions of various kinds. I do not blame anyone; instead, I want to share with you how addiction impacts the family system.

As I read this letter, you may experience a wide range of emotions, emotions like anxiety, confusion, shock, anger, or disgust. Regardless of your feelings, I want you to know it is okay to leave anytime—you do not need to sit here and listen to my story.

I too may have strong feelings coming over me as I read this letter. I want you to know that I will let myself feel and not hide behind a mask and pretend I have it all together.

I have learned that feelings are neither right nor wrong, good or bad. Feelings are just feelings, and it is okay to have them. In saying this, I want you to know it is safe to feel. Again, if you need to step out and take a break or simply leave, I promise I will not take it personally or be mad, offended, or upset.

So, with that said, I want to be clear with everyone: I did not bring you here today to blame or shame you. Mom and Dad, I realize you may feel embarrassed or responsible as I share my story. I want you to know that I am sharing my story to explain how I processed memories and what I have learned since then, not to make you feel bad or responsible.

I would also like to say that if anyone has any questions during this family impact letter reading, please stop me and let me know. Does anybody have any questions or concerns before I begin? Okay, if nobody has any questions, I'll move on.

I want to start by sharing my childhood memories from age seven. I remember, as a family, watching a movie together as we often did. There was a scene in the movie where the characters mentioned the name of a place where they were going. I believe it was a bar. I will share the name of that place with you, but I want you to know it is still awkward for me.

I also know it might be uncomfortable for you to hear it from me as you may not even remember—to the point you may laugh, and I get it. Still, I need to bring it up because this moment in my childhood represented a time when I was confused about what kind of content was acceptable and unacceptable for me to see and hear.

As I remember, the place in the movie was called "Ta-Tas and More." Even as a forty-two-year-old man, it's awkward to use that phrase in front of you because we didn't use that vocabulary in the family. You can only imagine my curiosity as a seven-year-old hearing that phrase; naturally, I asked the question that any child that age might ask. "What does Ta-Tas mean?" As I remember, everyone laughed and was told not to say those words or ask ever again. As a result, I remember feeling embarrassed, chastised, and confused all at the same time.

Now, to be clear, I wasn't allowed to watch scenes with nudity, and if anything ever came up, I remember being told to quickly look away if there was anything I felt was inappropriate. However, as I remember some of the movies we watched together as a family, there were a lot of sexually themed material. I want you all to know it was difficult to discern what was okay to watch, let alone process what I was subjected to. Do I look away and pretend not to notice? Do I look and act as if it is no big deal? Do I ask questions risking that I would be laughed at? Do I take the risk of getting in trouble? It was all very confusing to me.

Around age seven, maybe until nine years old, there were a couple of kids at school who were boyfriend-girlfriends, but I was still at an age where I was disinterested because I thought girls still had cooties. I remember being teased by the family about whether I wanted to have girl-friends, which was embarrassing and made me want a girlfriend even less.

Still, around this time, Mom and Dad, I remember watching your marital relationship dynamics, which was very confusing. Before I share more, I want you to know I am not blaming you but rather sharing how I was impacted.

As I recall, there were times when you were upset with each other but teased each other, trying to get a kiss or a hug, which was confusing. I grew to believe that a marital couple could hurt each other with their words and actions but not have to talk about it afterward. The modeling to me was not having to talk about it. I learned it was okay to hurt someone you loved but never have to take responsibility for it.

I also learned it was acceptable and normal for married people to talk about how attractive "others" are. Being taught to look for attractive traits in others seemed to be our family's norm.

Examples I grew up with were, "oh, she has nice legs" or "look at his biceps" or hearing that "he should have been my boyfriend" or "she should have been my girlfriend." This was from within our own family and from most of our extended family members.

These teachings played a significant role in my concept of marriage. As confusing as it was, I do remember having a sense that my idea of marriage was when two people love each other, they need to commit to one another to only date and support each other. As I write this, I can still feel the disturbance in my body to what I witnessed and felt deep in my heart. This added a level of confusion to my concept of marriage growing up.

At age nine, I had a dog named Patches. As you may remember, Patches was my best pal. He helped me feel comforted in a world where I was starting to feel more alone. As I recall, Mom, you had just started a new job, and, Dad, you were working more overtime. Sandy, you had already moved out of the house to live with a friend. Cathy, you were busy with sports and school. So having Patches was helpful for me in this transition, and he helped me feel not so alone.

Unfortunately, one day, while I was at school, somebody ran over Patches with their car, and he died. Mom, Dad, when I got home, I was told Patches had run away. Before I read more, I want both of you to know I believe you meant well by telling me this. I also know it must have been hard for both of you as I leaned out of the car window, being driven around the neighborhood, calling out his name—knowing he was already dead. Deep inside, though, I knew Patches was gone too, but I held on, wishing he wasn't.

When both of you told me the truth, I was very angry with both of you for allowing me to get my hopes up. It was easier for me to be mad than to experience the deep pain and sorrow that came from losing my best friend because I missed him so much.

I bring up Patches's passing because I realize now that I was so absorbed with grief and not knowing how to process the loss that I began to rebel silently. This was when things started to really change for me.

I started keeping secrets and purposely keeping things from all of you. I began creating a double life. One part of my life was just being a kid, funny and goofy, while the other side of me was living in rebellion and hurt.

I ended my friendship with Scott, Tony, and Dave shortly after Patches died. I formed new friends with Curt and the others known as the Fister Gang. They were not a good choice of friends for me because they tended to cause trouble in and out of school.

Not long after hanging out with those guys, I was kicked off the safety patrol, student council, and peer mediators for being disruptive in school. Of course, I kept this from all of you. As terrible as I felt about rebelling, what would hurt even more was if these guys rejected me. I felt that everyone was against me, as dysfunctional as they all were. I had to fit in somewhere.

At age eleven, I remember it was cool to have girlfriends. During this time, I mustered enough courage and asked a girl if she wanted to be my girlfriend. Sadly, I was turned down. I felt so embarrassed. Though embarrassed, I somehow thought I was fitting in simply by trying.

I remember watching many movies on TV and listening to the radio more than ever. I was starting to surround myself with sexualized music videos on MTV and rap music on the radio. Lori and Barb, you might even remember I had a favorite song one year called the thong song, which was not a wholesome choice of music, but it was "in" at the time. Although the music videos did not have nudity in them, I remember being excited by them due to the sexually suggestive themes contained within them.

I was intrigued by a restaurant called Hooters because they had very sexually dressed females in tight tops and tight shorts. During a trip to Hooters with Jake, Cathy's friend, I felt privileged because I was doing something other kids talked about but had not done before. I remember this was an opportunity to brag to my friends, trying to fit in.

Around the same age, I attended a "Teen Night" event. I remember going with the Fister Gang. It was a club for eighteen and under. I remember seeing one of my friends "make out" with a girl there, which was weird because I typically did not watch movie scenes that showed two people kissing. However, this experience was different because it was live right before me. Without feeling awkward, I tried to act cool. In retrospect, I had wished I had someone to talk to who could help me process this experience and what was to be expected at this age of sexual development.

During this same event, an older boy who knew some of my gang friends showed us how to

look up girl's skirts. One particular girl was danc-
ing on the stage, and we tried to see up her dress.
I honestly felt it was wrong and looked away. As
I recall, I was more upset with my friends than
being aroused sexually. I wasn't at that point yet,
but looking back, I realize it was not a good environment or friends I happened to be drawn to
just to fit in.

As time passed, I started to feel more comfortable liking girls but not comfortable telling
the family I was interested in girls. Instead, I
would say to everyone that I liked famous models
or pop stars, which was my way of avoiding the
discomfort of being teased or laughed into dating. It was easier to admit liking famous people,
knowing I would never be with than to admit
liking someone at school.

When I was twelve or so, I remember
attending a sex education talk at my middle
school by one of my male teachers. I remember
going, but I do not remember much as everyone
laughed and made fun of everything being talked
about. Truth be known, I was totally embarrassed
for not knowing this ahead of time.

At age thirteen, I was learning more about
dating. I knew that kids not only kissed but also
touched each other's "private parts" and sometimes would even have sex.

I remember it became a trend to have a con-
dom in our wallets. To fit in and be cool, I got
one from a friend and carried it for a short time
even though I did not know what it was or how
to use it. I only knew it had something to do
with sex.

I still did not really understand what sex
was, but I knew that it was best to be experi-

enced between two married adults. We discussed nothing specifically as a family, but I think it was implied in conversations.

It was during this age I learned from my peers what masturbation meant. Even the sexualized TV and music that I listened to did not help explain masturbation, but I know it was popular in almost every area of life. I remember getting bits and pieces from friends but never fully understood what it meant or how to do it. I once again felt unprepared and foolish for not knowing. I did not learn what was okay or not okay to do. I believed it was up to me to figure this sex thing out.

During middle school, I was getting picked on a lot. I was body-shamed due to my underdeveloped body. I felt degraded. It was painful. To be honest, I still struggle today as a forty-two-year-old man. This is why I never took my shirt off at pool parties or the beach; I was too embarrassed about the fatty tissue on my chest and didn't want anyone to notice.

Looking back, I believe the reason that I never talked about bullying was that I was struggling with feeling somewhat responsible as I rarely exercised. I also felt embarrassed by my weight. I know I struggled with believing maybe all of you felt the same way about me as the kids at school since there were times when, as a family, you teased me about being chubby or clumsy or about my lack of athletic abilities.

I became very guarded and did what I could to hide from everyone. It was lonely to live like that, but I felt I had no other choice. I bring this up because I realized, looking back, that these deep feelings of shame and loneliness were something that I did not know how to process healthily.

Around age fourteen, I was exposed to something that would forever change how I viewed dating, sex, and marriage. One day in class, a friend of mine showed me some pornographic images on the computer. I remember seeing the female body in its entirety. It was the first time I actually saw people having sex. I saw varying sexual positions and acts people did. I remember it felt wrong, but at the same time, I felt drawn to it.

I became sexually interested and curious. As a result, I started to look for pornography secretly on our home computer. It became apparent the home computer provided endless access. The behavior became a habit, and I found myself searching for pornographic material more frequently and for more extended periods of time.

When I viewed pornography, I felt a sense of escape from the ongoing teasing at school. I was trying to medicate the shame and loneliness that came from being teased, and the pornography fueled a fantasy life where I felt I was admired, respected, and nurtured.

During this time, I was trying to create a sense of masculinity that the teasing had stolen from me. Still, ironically, pornography made me even more insecure about my body image due to comparing my own body to that of the male porn stars I saw. I had begun to see and understand sex as a performance. It was about the orgasm. I knew it was wrong to view pornography, and I was too afraid to talk to anyone for fear of getting in trouble.

Later that year, I discovered that while viewing pornography, it was pleasurable to touch my penis. Although I didn't have a word for it at the time, I would later figure out that it was called masturbation. As a fourteen-year-old, it was awkward, and I knew I would not discuss it with anyone. I believed it was not safe for me to do so.

At home, I was starting to become even more isolated as I tried to find time alone to look at pornography. I remember staying up until everyone was asleep to find TV shows or get on the computer.

Other times, I would read my truck magazines just to see and "clip" racy pictures of women I found and hid them in my room. Living like that was exhausting, but I was trying to hide it and willing to go to more extraordinary lengths just to get the escape I needed.

Within this same year, I felt like porn and masturbation were not enough to provide the kind of escape I was looking for. Internet chat rooms and instant message apps were starting to emerge. I used them to overcome my social anxiety and fear of rejection. Before starting high school, I began to go online and exercise my hip-hop skills by getting into rap battles in chat rooms as a means to find something of a sexual nature.

I remember meeting many people through the chat rooms. One female I met seemed interested in me, so I chatted with her more privately. Eventually, that chat developed into an online relationship, and we called each other once, but ultimately, the relationship fizzled out. I believe I intended to have phone sex with her. Fortunately, nothing further happened. I guess she lost interest and moved on.

Later that summer, I got an AOL instant messenger account and discovered I could talk to girls who were friends with my friends from school. I remember becoming interested in one girl who seemed promiscuous. She lived close by, so we decided to meet each other. Fortunately, it did not work out, so we never "hooked up."

I was a loose cannon with no end in sight as I had begun to sexualize females as if they were all porn stars. I objectified them and saw them as sexual objects rather than seeing them as people who had dignity and personhood. My online and offline behavior eventually became unmanageable.

Mom, around age fifteen, I believe you found pornographic material on our home computer. It was during a get-together you and Dad were hosting and confronted me (not sure why you used the computer during a get-together, but you did). I am sure the search belonged to me, but I denied my problem and avoided taking responsibility. Barb and Lori, I even tried to blame it on one of you, and that was wrong of me. I shouldn't have done that. I am sorry.

Another time I remember getting caught was when you, Mom, found the stash of racy pictures from my truck magazines in my room and tried to get me to confess. Rather than concede, I looked for the quickest and fastest way to get rid of them when you weren't looking to avoid any further conversation. So, even though I didn't realize it at the time, I was getting used to lying and setting my course toward a life of addictive behaviors.

The secrets, the lies, the shame, the knowing it's wrong but doing it anyway, the medicating of wounds such as my own insecurity and low self-esteem issues, the increased amount of time I spent online, the searching for new pornographic material each time, the getting caught and being confronted—these were all major warning signs. Beyond that, I became more forgetful, a hallmark of mine as a young man. I think many of you may remember the pool overflowing and forgetting to do chores? I have come to understand these too were signs that I was preoccupied with my addiction.

Around age sixteen, I started slimming down after joining a boxing gym. While the teasing at school stopped, I was still really insecure. Boxing was beginning to give me confidence in my capabilities. I made friends from high school through boxing and enjoyed the challenge and companionship. Still, one weekend, I went with those friends to a boxing match out of town, and something happened to me there that was very traumatic.

During the trip, I stayed in a hotel room with one other guy I boxed with and his grandfather, who was a chaperone. It had two queen beds and no couch, so I ended up sharing a bed with the other guy. Of course, that was awkward, two guys on one bed, but I think we just put pillows in the middle and slept on opposite sides.

In the middle of the night, I woke up to this guy sticking his hand down my pants to touch my butt, and I quickly smacked his hand away. I remember feeling shocked, angry, and confused. This guy just touched me! I was also disgusted and embarrassed. I immediately rolled onto the floor and slept there for the rest of the night.

I didn't know if this guy was doing this in his sleep or if he was trying to make a move on me; regardless, I did not want to talk about it to anyone. It took me ten years before I finally said anything to anyone. Even though this was an isolated event, it is still a sensitive area for me. Even today, if Patty tries to touch my butt without asking permission, I still react negatively because of this past abusive experience.

As a result of this, I felt even more motivated to prove my manhood and my desire for the opposite sex. It propelled my addiction and objectification of women to a more public arena.

During this time, I truly began seeking my faith journey. I could not bring myself to talk about it, but I felt Jesus was ringing true to me, and I received him into my life because I was so entangled in my addiction. I knew I needed a savior, and here was a God who, despite all my sins, past, present, and future, had died for me to be free from sin and shame. I knew I needed him!

Faith One was the first place to ever explain that to me, and I found hope in that. Still, I remember having the chance to talk about my addiction during one of my Men of Faith group experiences. However, I was still too ashamed to be honest about it because I felt like nobody else struggled the way that I did. Church, for me, provided an escape, and I found myself less interested in pornography and more interested in going out with my new church friends.

Steve, I want you to know that you positively influenced me during this time of life. I appreciate the time we spent fishing and playing basketball together. You helped me experience a sense of peace, which was a healthy diversion from the addiction. I believe these times together helped me take the poster of the woman in the bikini off my wall. I felt like I was becoming a new person even though I was still struggling with the uncontrollable urges to view porn, objectify women, and masturbate.

At age eighteen and just starting college, I started to have girlfriends, and it was the time I first had my sexual experience with another person. I felt conflicted because I was becoming a Christian, and I did not want to be sexual. However, the temptation was too strong for me to say no. I believe it also was because I was battling a sex addiction.

Another challenge was not knowing how to handle the newfound freedom and lack of accountability from not living at home anymore. I found that the sexual experiences I had in college lessened my desire for pornography and masturbation. Sex with another person was now the higher need and fix.

It was during my college years that I met Patty. Though I was in a relationship with her, I was still very active in my addiction, which I kept from her. The rationale I used was that I was not cheating on her because I felt if I could look and only fantasize, it wasn't the same as cheating.

I further rationalized this by the earlier modeling experiences I witnessed in the family. It was normal and expected to find others attractive, even outside a relationship or marriage. Although I still felt it was wrong, I did it anyway. After all, I did not want to lose Patty, so I had to hide this from her.

A few months into dating, Patty stumbled upon some questionable searches on my computer about sex, and I remember when she asked what they were, I was so afraid and so embarrassed. I knew I was caught, and there was no way around it since I was the only one who used that computer.

Ultimately, I told her that they were pornographic searches that I had made. Still, instead of giving her the truth, I said to her that it was something I did in the past and wasn't doing anymore. I purposely lied to her; sadly, she believed all my lies. I knew she was concerned about my sexual unhealthiness and even tried to help me by getting help from other guys she felt were healthy.

Patty introduced me to some guys involved in a men's ministry group at school. I joined, but it took me a while before I opened up. I always kept some level of secrecy about my addiction because I was not ready to let anyone see and know the real me.

As time passed, my relationship with Patty became strained as I continued to flirt with other women, even in front of her. When she confronted me, I was very harsh toward her. On top of that, I was not making any movement toward committing to her, and we were on the brink of not making it.

After three years of dating, I proposed to Patty because I knew I loved her and everything about her. I did not want to lose her. All the while, the addiction was still active. I thought that maybe if we married and had sex frequently, then my desire for the addiction would stop, but it didn't.

As everyone knows, at age twenty-eight, we got married and moved to Wisconsin. That was because Ford was the only place to give me a job. It was also close to a law school Patty wanted to attend to further her career.

We found a church, and after a few months, I openly confessed my sin, my sin of addiction. That was scary for me because I knew I had plenty of sin buried in my life, and I was afraid that I would need to confess it at some point in front of the church.

After a few months, we started seeing a couple's counselor at the church. Although I stopped viewing pornography, I was still actively objectifying women, and I would fantasize about them often. I would stalk them at work and even masturbate in the bathroom at work. Patty and the counselor never knew this as I kept it hidden.

I had grown cold and harsh toward Patty. I didn't know how to handle the stresses of life, so I placed a lot of blame and pressure on her, displacing my feelings. I was absent and did not give her the affection and care she needed. Things were getting worse maritally, and one day, I felt so much guilt and regret that I decided I was going to talk to her openly about my addiction.

I called the pastor and his wife, our counselor, told them what was happening, and told them I would talk with Patty about it. About six months into marriage, I told Patty I had a problem. We met at an office with the pastor and our counselor. I remember the pastor told me that I just needed to stop my behavior, and he told Patty she needed to forgive me.

The pastor caused further harm and abuse to Patty by telling her that she just needed to get over it and forgive me, and that was abusive because she had to deny her own experience in what is known as betrayal partner trauma. As a result, Patty was shocked, confused, and devastated. However, given the circumstances, she could still support me as best as possible.

The truth was I was not fully transparent with the pastor, our counselor, or Patty as I still hid the details that some of the women I objectified were church members.

This later caused us to leave the church and lose the support system that we had just built. I also spared the details that throughout our college years, I was actively engaged in objectification, pornography, and masturbation. I also caused Patty to give up the dear friendships that were special to her.

Soon after my confession, I felt some relief, and I began to admit to Patty daily if I had objectified women at work, which was a frequent occurrence.

Because I was still in denial, Patty continued to be abused by me, hoping I would not relapse again. Due to the gravity of my addiction, we were referred to a few different therapists and support groups who honestly caused more harm than good.

It seemed as if everyone tried to normalize my addiction and were operating on an old couple's therapy model that people who marry people with an addiction are automatically seen as codependents.

My attempt to deal with my sexual behavior traumatized Patty even more because I allowed the blame to be put on her. Even though I was relieved that some pressure was taken off me, I let Patty experience continued trauma and abuse.

Truth is I did not own my addiction as I should have. I still continued to lie to Patty as she did not know the full extent of my addiction. To be clear, although I allowed her to be blamed, I, not her, was the problem. Patty is not responsible in any way for my addiction since I was an addict long before I even knew her.

Furthermore, Patty did not enable my behavior in any way, shape, or form. I also used this archaic codependent model as a way to blame Patty for our marital issues and resisted taking responsibility for the trauma that I was causing.

It was not long after joining the various support groups that I went back into hiding my addiction. I thought that if I tried hard enough or at least sought the help of sober people, I could achieve sobriety, but I never did. I lived in denial and deceit.

My abusive ways toward Patty continued, even after all the carnage I caused. I did not consider what she was going through. I abandoned Patty emotionally because I didn't want to deal with the hurt that I had caused her. Though, in her gut, Patty knew something was wrong, I denied her reality. I had created so many lies. I wove a cobweb of lies that were too big to manage.

One way I attempted to manage the unmanageability was to purposely try to talk her out of the reality that something was wrong. That is called gaslighting.

I further traumatized Patty with my gaslighting behavior. As a result of all of this, I caused Patty to develop complex post-traumatic stress disorder (c-PTSD), panic attack disorder, and anxiety, which caused her to have suicide ideations.

I will stop there momentarily because that's a lot to digest. I want you to know that I am sharing this to help explain how bad my addiction has gotten. You may feel enraged, like how could I cause this sweet girl so much pain? I want you all to know I was wrong. I was focused on my own needs. I was choosing to take an unhealthy path and attempting to medicate my way through life. I took the easy road, yet Patty stuck by my side through it all.

About five years later, things started to stabilize, or so I thought, when Patty and I were buying our first house.

It was not long afterward Patty again found some sexually themed pictures on my cell phone. As any addict would do, they would lie and say it was not theirs. Although I felt guilt, shame, and fear, I did not come clean with her.

I continued in my addiction for another nine months before, again, the shame and guilt grew to the point where I decided to confess to Patty that I still had the problem and that I needed more help.

At this point, my addiction had escalated even more, which grew to be more than beyond looking at women in sexual ways. It escalated to going online to look for women on a dating website.

During this time, I also made Internet searches for strip clubs and the legality of prostitution in the US. Although still attending church, I was objectifying women and even minors.

I was spiraling downward, and you might be sitting there in disbelief, but I am here today to say that that was the reality of what my life had become.

I am sharing this to let you know how my addiction took me to depths I did not think I was capable of. I had become the extreme of Dr. Jekyll and Mr. Hyde. In my Dr. Jekyll persona, I was happy and funny to the outside world, even preaching from the pulpit and leading recovery groups. In my private life, I was living as Mr. Hyde.

When I finally disclosed this to Patty again, I was still vague and purposely minimizing my addictive behavior. I still valued protecting myself at the expense of abusing Patty.

When the bottom hit, I knew that I needed professional help. I was referred to an outpatient recovery practice in Michigan. I began my treatment for addiction recovery at NorthPoint Professional Counseling. Although my addiction was still very much alive, I started my recovery program. It was during this early time in recovery I created an exit plan just in case Patty were to leave me. I created a plan B just in case.

Months into my recovery program, I continued to sexually relapse and hide my sexual behaviors from my therapist, John, and Patty. I was not fully surrendered as I had built so many walls up to avoid feeling shame and despair.

As part of my recovery program, I had to pass a polygraph examination. The polygraph was the only way I could prove I had really changed and was not actively lying about my addictive behaviors. It took years of trying to pass my polygraph due to many reasons, one of which was my lack of maturity. In fact, it took me five years into the recovery program to finally pass. My verifiable sobriety date is August 10, 2019.

My recovery program has been much more than just getting sober; it has been about creating and maintaining my health in every aspect of life. Part of what I had to learn was to trust the counsel of others to help me. I now have a sponsor whom I call five days a week. I have a weekly men's recovery support group led by my therapist, John, and weekly individual sessions with him as well.

As much as I wanted to get through this quickly, I had to learn that there was no magic pill, just that I needed to work my recovery steps every day consistently. I had to learn how to surrender and submit to the process. I had to be consistent in keeping up with the program's momentum. I had to learn how to create healthy boundaries to help me be safe from my addiction. I had to understand what I watched on TV or in movies. I had to evaluate healthy and unhealthy influences in my life. I had to assess what was/is beneficial for me and what was not helpful for me. I had to create healthy boundaries to protect myself from my addiction.

An example of this is that if I am watching something on TV, I will turn it off if I notice something unhealthy for me to see. Another example is when someone wants to share a joke or share a picture with me, I first will ask what it is so I am not triggered.

As a recovering addict, I had to overcome the struggle of setting healthy boundaries because it felt as if I was depriving myself of an everyday life. I thought, *Why can't I watch whatever I want to on TV?* What I had to learn was what things triggered my addiction and what kind of life I truly wanted.

I also learned how to create healthy boundaries around my self-care. An example of my restorative self-care is ensuring I exercise, get a good sleep, and create balance in my life.

I also had to learn how to create a balance between my finances and my time. This is important as I would expense myself to the point where I could not healthily handle life situations. These boundaries were difficult because I felt unworthy of love and undeserving due to all I had done.

My addiction had caused me to be comfortable in chaos and stress. As ironic as it may seem, addiction relies on chaos and stress to survive.

In recovery, I learned what positive sexuality and courtship disorders were. I learned to embrace the recovery essentials and how to apply them in my everyday life.

Although I still struggle with black-and-white thinking at times, I had to learn that sex was a gift from God and had to learn how to experience it as he designed. I had to start thinking about how sex was a healthy thing within the constraints of my marriage.

Overall, I am relearning how to experience life in a healthy way. Not everything I did was wrong; I had to inventory the things I wanted to change and start making the necessary changes. I needed to keep challenging myself and letting healthy people around me hear my story, know my thoughts, and know my feelings so they could help me.

This letter is to help you know the real me. My letter is to show you my flaws and weakness. I hope you can learn from my experiences.

You may be sitting there thinking this is out of character for me, and all of this is surreal. I assure you it is not; every word I have spoken is true.

I have learned my true identity is that I am a son of God. I am compassionate, creative, and courageous. Still, I know that I am always one decision away from going back into my addiction. So I embrace my recovery and journey toward a positive life of healthiness and sobriety.

In closing, Patty was a victim of this. She went through hell and lost so much to be here with me today. Patty is a heroine. It might sound cliché, but I genuinely believe it is because she allowed God to use her in ways that enabled her to be here.

I want to end by thanking all of you for allowing me to share myself with you today. I want to share that if anyone can relate to this, you need to break free from denial and get help. You do not need to take anything of unhealthiness to your grave. It is not yours to carry. Get professional help and learn to give it to Jesus! It doesn't have to be something sexual or even have to do with addiction. If you are struggling with woundedness, abuse, or trauma, I want you to know there is help.

If you have any questions, I am open to sharing anything anytime. I am an open book. So, with that said, I invite you to share any comments, concerns, or questions with me or John.
I love you all.

Mark

Chapter 6
History of Fear

Growing up with fear can profoundly impact an individual's development, emotional well-being, and overall outlook on life. Fear is a natural and necessary emotion that helps us respond to threats and danger. However, when fear becomes a constant or overwhelming presence during one's formative years, it can lead to challenges and long-term consequences.

Research on fear and the brain is a broad and interdisciplinary field encompassing neuroscience, psychology, and other related disciplines. Although it is not the scope of this book to dive deep into fear and its effects on the brain, I believe parents would benefit from some basic knowledge.

Understanding how the brain processes and responds to fear is crucial for understanding various human behavior and mental health aspects. Below, I'll provide an overview of some key areas of research on fear and the brain:

The amygdala is a small almond-shaped structure deep within the brain that plays a central role in processing fear and emotional responses. Research has shown that damage to the amygdala can result in a lack of fear and impaired recognition of fearful facial expressions.

Studies have examined how the brain learns to associate specific stimuli or situations with fear. Classical conditioning experiments, often involving animals like rats, have provided insights into the neural mechanisms underlying fear learning and memory.

Researchers have explored the role of various neurotransmitters and hormones in the regulation of fear. For example, the neurotransmitter serotonin has been implicated in fear-related disorders, such as anxiety.

Advances in neuroimaging techniques, such as functional magnetic resonance imaging (fMRI) and positron emission tomography (PET), have allowed scientists to observe the brain's activity during fear processing. These studies have highlighted the involvement of multiple brain regions, including the prefrontal cortex and the insula.

Understanding how fear can be unlearned or extinguished is a significant area of research. This has implications for the treatment of anxiety disorders, such as post-traumatic stress disorder (PTSD). Researchers study the neural mechanisms involved in fear extinction processes.

Research has investigated how both genetic and environmental factors contribute to an individual's vulnerability to fear and anxiety disorders. Twin studies and genetic research have identified specific genes and genetic variations associated with fear-related conditions.

Studies have explored the use of medications to modulate the brain's fear response. For instance, medications like selective serotonin reuptake inhibitors (SSRIs) are commonly prescribed for anxiety disorders.

Much research focuses on understanding the neurological basis of PTSD, which is characterized by a heightened and prolonged fear response following a traumatic event. This work aims to develop better treatments and interventions for individuals with PTSD.

Investigating the neural circuits that control fear responses is a central aspect of research. This includes understanding the connections between different brain regions involved in processing fear and the role of specific neural pathways.

Researchers have explored various therapeutic interventions, such as cognitive-behavioral therapy and exposure therapy, for treating fear and anxiety-related disorders. These therapies often involve modifying the brain's response to fear-inducing stimuli.

Constant exposure to fear can lead to heightened anxiety and stress. Children who grow up in fearful environments may develop chronic anxiety disorders, which can affect their ability to cope with everyday challenges.

Living in a fearful environment can make it difficult to regulate one's emotions. Fear may lead to mood swings, irritability, and difficulty forming stable relationships.

Children who experience fear regularly may develop low self-esteem and a negative self-image. They may internalize the fear and believe they are inherently unworthy or unlovable.

Growing up with fear often leads to constant alertness, making relaxing or trusting others challenging. This hypervigilance can lead to difficulties in forming trusting relationships.

Chronic fear can lead to various physical health problems, including high blood pressure, a weakened immune system, and an increased risk of heart disease.

People who grow up with fear may develop maladaptive coping mechanisms, such as substance abuse, self-harm, or unhealthy relationships, as a way to deal with their emotions.

Fear can hinder a child's cognitive and emotional development. It may affect their ability to learn, concentrate, and explore new experiences.

Fear can impact a person's ability to build and maintain healthy relationships. They may struggle with trust, intimacy, and communication.

In some cases, individuals who grow up with fear may perpetuate this cycle by creating fearful environments for their children. The intergenerational transmission of fear is a complex issue that can perpetuate the negative effects.

It's important to note that growing up with fear doesn't necessarily mean a person will experience all of these consequences. Everyone's experience is unique, and factors such as the severity and duration of the fear, the presence of supportive adults, and individual resilience all play a role in shaping the outcomes.

Research on fear and the brain is ongoing, and new discoveries continually expand our understanding of how the brain processes and regulates fear. This knowledge can lead to better treatments and interventions for individuals with fear and anxiety-related conditions.

Addressing the effects of growing up with fear often involves therapy, counseling, and support from trusted individuals. Recognizing the impact of fear and seeking help can be the first step toward healing and developing healthier coping mechanisms to navigate life's challenges.

To better understand the impact of fear on the child's developing brain, I have provided four client introspections regarding how fear has shaped their life.

Meet Ken. Ken presented a composed and confident demeanor with his neatly pressed suits and well-groomed appearance. However, beneath this facade, Ken grappled with a tapestry of fears that shaped the contours of his life.

Ken writes:

> As I reflect on early memories of fear, I think about learning to follow the rules or experiencing Mom and Dad being mad, resulting in punishment.
>
> There was a time when my Dad lost his temper and whipped me with a studded belt. That experience left such an impact that I became extremely fearful of him. The lesson I learned was to never upset or disappoint my Dad.
>
> Another incident was a deep fear of trusting authority after my parents lied to me about the death of my dog. This fear led to my silent rebellion and was coupled with anger, fear, resentment, and grief.
>
> Flooded by such heavy emotions, I did not know where to turn to process. As a result, I became rebellious and surrounded myself with unhealthy friends. Ironic as it was, I took my unprocessed and unresolved feelings and found friends who also had unsolved feelings of anger, fear, hurt, and resentment.
>
> I lived this way for decades, fearing that people close to me would reject or punish me if I upset or disappoint them. My anger and fear also

led me to avoid taking responsibility for my hurtful, abusive behaviors, causing further isolation.

Because of my unresolved issues with fear, I created increased strife in my relationships and increased internal dissonance because I was displeased with my wrongdoing and immoral life choices, all of which left me living a life of secrecy, pain, and hurt.

Meet Susan. Susan was a spirited young woman in her twenties. Susan was a kaleidoscope of contradictions due to growing up with fear. Susan had difficulties navigating the complex terrain of adulthood with a blend of enthusiasm and uncertainty.

Susan writes:

My childhood was marked by the echoes of fear lingering in the hallways of my family's home. My parents struggled with their own demons and were haunted by their past, which unwittingly passed on the legacy of fear to me, their daughter.

As far back as I can remember, my home's atmosphere was always thick with tension. Raised voices, slamming doors, and tear-streaked faces were common sights. My parents, scarred by their own traumatic experiences, found solace in the shadows of their fears. Unbeknownst to them, their fears cast long shadows over my early formative years.

My father, haunted by memories of his turbulent childhood, carried the fear of abandonment like a heavy burden. His insecurities manifested in an overprotective nature, often smothering him with rules and restrictions. He feared letting me go, convinced that the world beyond his front door was fraught with danger.

On the other hand, my mother, a survivor of domestic violence, harbored a deep-seated fear of vulnerability. She erected emotional walls to shield herself from the pain of the past, making it challenging for me to connect with her on a close level. I craved my mother's affection but was met with an impenetrable barrier of fear.

As I navigated my teenage years, the effects of her upbringing became more apparent. Fear had woven itself into the fabric of her identity, giving rise to insecurities that manifested in various aspects of her life.

I had fears of rejection, which led me to avoid social situations. I doubted my worthiness of genuine connections, convinced that others would eventually abandon me, just as my father had feared abandonment.

My mother's fear of vulnerability translated into my fear of failure. The prospect of not meeting expectations paralyzed me with self-doubt. The pressure to excel became a constant source of anxiety, which affected my grades in school.

My parents, unintentionally modeling dysfunctional relationships, left me grappling with a fear of intimacy. Opening up emotionally felt like exposing myself to potential pain, which left me unable to trust others with my true feelings.

As I reached adulthood, I realized the need to confront the shadows of my fears. With the support of a compassionate therapist, I began unraveling the layers of insecurity that had taken root in my psyche.

Through introspection and guided healing, I learned to differentiate my fears from those of my parents. I discovered the strength to challenge limiting beliefs and redefine my self-worth.

Slowly but surely, I emerged from the shadows of fear, cultivating resilience and embracing the possibility of a life not dictated by insecurity.

I hope my journey serves as a testament to the transformative power of self-awareness and the courage to confront the ghosts of one's past.

Meet Rachel. Rachel is a woman in her midthirties whose life had been intricately shaped by fear's silent but omnipresent force. Her journey is a testament to the profound impact that fear can have on an adult's life trajectory.

Racheal writes:

My childhood was marked by unpredictability and insecurity. Growing up in a tumultuous household where financial struggles and parental discord were frequent companions, fear became a constant presence. The instability of my formative years planted the seeds of anxiety and apprehension that would linger well into my adulthood.

In pursuing stability and security, I made conservative choices in my academic and professional endeavors. Fear of failure and financial instability guided my decisions, leading me to a steady but uninspiring career path. The allure of pursuing my true passions took a backseat to the perceived safety of a conventional job.

Fear extended into my relationships. My fear of vulnerability, born out of witnessing the vulnerability of my parents, hindered my ability to form deep connections.

Intimacy became a source of anxiety, as opening up emotionally felt like exposing myself to potential pain. As a result, I maintained a certain emotional distance in my friendships and romantic relationships.

My fear created a self-imposed cage, limiting myself to the exploration of new experiences and ventures. Dreams I once harbored were deemed too risky, and the fear of the unknown kept me from pursuing the things that could bring fulfillment and joy.

Physically, fear took a toll on my overall well-being. Chronic stress, a by-product of my constant apprehension, manifested in both mental and physical health issues. The fear of the future, of not being able to meet societal expectations, contributed to a cycle of anxiety and stress.

As I approached my late thirties, a realization dawned upon me—the very fear that I thought was keeping me safe had, in fact, confined me. I decided to confront my fears head-on, seeking therapy to untangle the web of anxieties that had entwined my life.

Through therapy, I learned to reframe my relationship with fear. Instead of viewing it as an obstacle, I saw it as a signal, guiding me toward areas needing attention and growth. With newfound courage, I started taking small steps outside my comfort zone, pursuing passions I had long neglected.

As I embraced change, my life began to transform. I pursued further education in a field I was genuinely passionate about, allowing me to break free from the confines of my previous career. My relationships deepened as I learned to courageously navigate vulnerability, fostering connections that brought joy and support.

My journey was not without challenges; my story is about resilience and empowerment. Once

a shaping force in my life, fear became a catalyst for growth and self-discovery. As an adult, I
found the strength to rewrite my narrative and
redefine my relationship with fear, transforming
it from a limiting force into a guiding compass
for a more authentic and fulfilling life.

Lastly, let's meet Dave. Fear had clung to him from a young age
like a persistent shadow. His fear had its roots in a childhood marked
by constant change. Moving from place to place, Dave found solace
in the familiar confines of his home.

As he grew older, the fear of the unknown outside those familiar walls intensified. He hesitated to explore new places, meet new
people, or try new things. The safety of his routine became a security
blanket, shielding him from the uncertainties of the outside world.

Dave writes:

Fear has been my constant companion since
my youth. Growing up, I was taught to fear the
world outside my home. Fear was in the chaos
and unpredictability within my house. Fear was
in the chaos and unpredictability of school. Fear
was even in my church; I imagined religious per-
secution, displeasing God, going to hell, or losing
people I loved going to hell.

Since then, almost everything I've done has
been through the lens of fear. Sometimes, I've
run with it, welcoming it with reckless abandon,
as I willfully encounter dangerous people or situations. Other times, I'd be crippled by it, allowing it to consume my thoughts and fantasies. I've
conjured it in times of peace, seeking it in entertainment, media and/or friends. I wonder if I'm
afraid to be without fear.

Chapter 7
Pornography and Addiction

"Technology is transforming our sexuality."[1] The concept of pornography addiction is a subject of debate among experts in the fields of psychology, psychiatry, and neuroscience. Some professionals and organizations recognize it as a real and problematic condition while others are more skeptical.

Proponents of the idea that pornography addiction is real argue that some individuals may develop an unhealthy and compulsive relationship with pornography, similar to the way people can become addicted to substances like drugs or alcohol. They claim this can lead to negative consequences in various aspects of a person's life, including relationships, work, and mental well-being.

Critics argue that there is not enough scientific evidence to definitively classify pornography addiction as a distinct disorder in the same way that substance addictions are classified. They suggest that the concept of pornography addiction may be better understood as a form of compulsive or impulsive behavior related to underlying psychological or emotional issues rather than a true addiction in the traditional sense.

Robert Weiss, author, educator, and clinical expert in the treatment of adult intimacy disorders and related addictions, writes that as our increasing technological interconnectivity has brought with it affordable, easy links to distracting, arousing sexual content and anonymous sex, addiction and mental health professionals are seeing

---

[1]   Patrick Carnes, Ph.D., *Facing the Shadow*, (Gentle Path Press).

a corresponding increase in the number of people struggling with sexual and romantic addictions.

Regardless of belief, pornography can be found in many forms across all areas of the Internet. Whether in pictures, videos, sculptures, drawings, anime, written words, posts, texts, social media, video games, movies, etc. So why the lure? To answer the question is to understand the various factors involved.

One reason is it provides anonymity. "Internet users are lulled into thinking that no one is watching what they are doing."[2]

Another reason is that it can be seductive. Seductive because it "allows the person to think of online sexual behavior as impersonal (it hurts no one). Rather than real life, it is thought of as more like a computer game—another in the panoply of virtual realities."[3]

A third reason is one of convenience. All that is required is a smart device with Internet access, typing a few words, and off you go. Online pornography requires little, if any, money, effort, or time spent in searching; it is only a click away. Anyone can access pornography from their home without even getting out of bed or having to get dressed, and access is available anywhere.[4]

A fourth reason is stimulation. "A strong case has emerged that [online pornography] is capable of going beyond [a person's] own biological limits. Neuroscientist Donald Hilton describes today's technology as a 'supranormal stimulus.' No partner can compete with the Internet. People get so stimulated that sex feels more real… than their actual lives."[5]

Pornography provides novelty and variety. The Internet provides easy access to a wide range of sexual content, offering novelty and variety. This constant novelty can lead to a phenomenon known as "sensitization," where individuals may need increasingly novel or extreme content to maintain the same level of arousal.

Pornography use can cause dopamine release. Pornography can trigger the release of dopamine in the brain, a neurotransmitter asso-

---

[2]   Ibid.

[3]   Ibid.

[4]   Ibid.

[5]   Ibid.

ciated with pleasure and reward. This neurochemical response can create a reinforcing loop where individuals seek out more pornography to experience the pleasurable feelings associated with dopamine release.

Like any other addiction, people may turn to pornography as a means of escaping from stress, anxiety, or other negative emotions. The fantasy world provided by pornography may serve as a temporary escape from real-life problems.

Over time, individuals may associate sexual arousal and gratification primarily with pornography, making it difficult for them to engage in real-life sexual experiences without the same stimuli.

Pornography and erectile dysfunction (ED) is a condition that is "commonly associated with older age, but the inability to get or maintain an erection can also affect younger men—even teens."[6]

There are various potential causes of erectile dysfunction in teens, and it's essential to approach this issue with sensitivity and a focus on seeking medical advice. Possible causes may include:

Psychological factors. Stress, anxiety, depression, and other mental health issues can contribute to erectile dysfunction in teens. Academic pressure, relationship problems, or body image concerns may also play a role.

Hormonal changes. During adolescence, the body has significant hormonal changes. Hormonal imbalances or fluctuations, such as those related to puberty, can impact sexual function.

Medication side effects. Some medications prescribed for other health conditions may have side effects that can affect sexual function.

Physical health issues. Certain medical conditions, such as diabetes or cardiovascular problems, can affect blood flow and contribute to erectile dysfunction.

---

[6] https://www.verywellhealth.com/erectile-dysfunction-in-teens-5198104.

Lifestyle factors. Unhealthy lifestyle habits, such as smoking, excessive alcohol consumption, or a lack of physical activity, can contribute to erectile dysfunction.

If a teenager is experiencing erectile dysfunction, it's crucial for them to consult with a health-care professional. A doctor can conduct a thorough evaluation to identify the underlying cause and recommend appropriate treatment or interventions. In many cases, lifestyle changes, counseling, or medical treatments may be effective in addressing the issue.

A 2021 study entitled "Associations between Online Pornography Consumption and Sexual Dysfunction in Young Men" concluded: "This prevalence of ED [erectile dysfunction] in young men is alarmingly high, and the results of this study suggest a significant association with [problematic pornography consumption] PPC."[7]

Pornography use may change the person's neuropathways. The brain is highly adaptable, and repeated exposure to certain stimuli, such as pornography, can lead to changes in neural pathways. This can contribute to the development of habits and compulsive behaviors.

Another reason is that there is a lack of regulations. Unlike other addictive substances or behaviors, there is often a lack of social stigma and legal regulation surrounding pornography consumption. This lack of external consequences may contribute to continued use.

It is estimated that there are over forty-two million adult websites on the Internet today. It is also reported that the average age at which a child accesses pornography is age eleven.

Leading national sexual addiction expert Patrick Carnes, PhD states that today, over 70 percent of sex addicts report having problematic online sexual behavior. Two-thirds of those engaged have such despair over their Internet activities that they have had suicidal thoughts.

---

[7] https://www.ncbi.nlm.nih.gov/pmc/articles/PMC8569536/.

Sexual acting out online has been shown to manifest in similar offline behavior. People who already were sex addicts find the Internet accelerates their problem. Those who start in online behavior quickly start to act out in new ways offline.

One of the pioneering researchers of this problem, the late Dr. Al Cooper, described online sexual behavior as the "crack cocaine" of sexual compulsivity.

"Given the widespread availability of sexually explicit materials online, Internet sex addiction is the most common form of problem online behavior among users."[8]

Scientific literature from the National Library of Medicine (NLM) reports that a 2022 study revealed that the probability of viewing Internet pornography among males is decidedly higher than among females for every age category, except for the youngest category, between seven and twelve years old. For this age category, 27 percent of girls used the Internet, and 25 percent of boys viewed pornographic websites. At first glance, this result can seem paradoxical; however, it is in line with the results of recent surveys, according to which the age of first contact with pornography is very similar for boys and girls. It is important to notice that the first visits on Internet websites with pornographic content are likely driven by curiosity and not factors directly related to sexual drive.[9]

Pornography Statistics[10]

- Over forty million Americans are regular visitors to porn sites. The average visit lasts six minutes and twenty-nine seconds.
- There are around forty-two million porn websites, which total about 370 million pages of porn.

---

8   K. S. Young, "Internet Sex Addiction: Risk Factors, Stages of Development, and Treatment," *American Behavioral Scientist, 52,* (2008): 21–37.

9   https://www.ncbi.nlm.nih.gov/pmc/articles/PMC8888374/.

10   https://www.missionfrontiers.org/issue/article/15-mind-blowing-statistics-about-pornography-and-the-church.

- The porn industry's annual revenue is more than the NFL, NBA, and MLB combined. It is also more than the combined revenues of ABC, CBS, and NBC.
- Around 47 percent of families in the United States reported that pornography is a problem in their homes.
- Pornography use increases the marital infidelity rate by more than 300 percent.
- Around 94 percent of children will see porn by the age of fourteen.
- Around 56 percent of American divorces involve one party having an "obsessive interest" in pornographic websites.
- Around 33 percent of women aged twenty-five and under search for porn at least once per month.
- Around 55 percent of married men and 25 percent of married women say they watch porn at least once a month.

Online Sexual Behavior Symptomologies[11]

- Having a preoccupation with sex on the Internet.
- Frequently engaging in sex on the Internet more often or for more extended periods of time than intended.
- Repeated unsuccessful efforts to control, cut back on, or stop engaging in sex on the Internet
- Restlessness or irritability when attempting to limit or stop engaging in sex on the Internet.
- Using sex on the Internet as a way of escaping from problems or relieving feelings such as helplessness, guilt, anxiety, or depression.
- Returning to sex on the Internet day after day in search of a more intense or higher-risk sexual experience.
- Lying to family members, therapists, or others to conceal involvement with sex on the Internet.
- Committing illegal sexual acts online (e.g., sending or downloading child pornography).

---

[11] www. iiTAP.com.

- Jeopardizing or losing a significant relationship, job, or educational or career opportunity because of online sexual behavior.
- Incurring significant financial consequences as a result of engaging in online sexual behavior.

Section 4
Healthy Sexual Focus

What our kids hear and see in today's culture is rarely a representation of healthy love. Selfish, lustful, and even abusive behavior is passed off as a love relationship. That is why, in a real sense, we must redefine to our kids what such a relationship actually is from a biblical perspective.

—Craig T. Owens

Parental downloading

Estimated time left: 1 hour and 0 seconds

C: reader//87953:downloading_healthy_sexual_focus

Chapter 8
Understanding Healthy Sexuality

As human beings, we are all sexual creatures. We remain sexual creatures throughout our life spans. However, at specific points in our life span, our sexuality (desire/interest) may change. Regardless of change, we all remain sexual creatures.

Each sexual phase of life we experience can provide growth and development to bring greater continued satisfaction to our sexual health.

We are all biologically wired to respond to sexual stimuli. Our sexuality is more than sex; it is about our feelings, thoughts, attractions, and behaviors, not only about who we are but also toward others.

Admittedly, defining healthy sexuality is a difficult task, as each culture, subculture, and individual difference accepts different standards of sexual health.[1] Adding to the difficulty is that there is very limited research devoted to the subject of sexual health. Suppose we rely on the world's teachings. In that case, it will emphasize teaching that "anything goes," which leaves it up to each individual to define for themselves what sexual health is—resulting in relativism.

The World Health Organization (WHO) defines sexual health as a state of physical, emotional, mental, and social well-being in relation to sexuality; it is not merely the absence of disease, dysfunction, or infirmity. Sexual health requires a positive and respectful approach to sexuality and sexual relationships, as well as the possibil-

---

[1] American Sexual Health Association.

ity of having pleasurable and safe sexual experiences free of coercion, discrimination, and violence.[2]

A 2020 study entitled "Innovation and Integration of Sexuality in Family Life Education" states that sexuality is a fundamental aspect of the human experience. Sexuality is experienced at every stage in the life span and intersects with feelings, experiences, and practices at all levels, from intrapersonal to interpersonal, social, and cultural. Further, sexuality is an important component of public health, individual health, and healthy families; educating about such a central aspect of life is both obvious and crucial. Sexuality encompasses a broad range of topics and dimensions, including physical, mental, and social well-being across the life course; further, sexuality is embedded in and influenced by interpersonal relationships, as well as by broader sociocultural values and beliefs.[3]

Sexuality is experienced at every stage in the life span.

Due to pornography use, faulty beliefs such as bias with males and females, skewed perceptions, intimacy, sexuality, and even commitment have become contaminated. No genre of pornography is useful or helpful in learning what healthy sexuality is.

Patrick Carnes, PhD, a leading expert in the field of sexual/pornography addiction, writes that in searching for what research has been done on sexual health, the answers are elusive. There is much more written about sex going awry. Research also gets obscured by the politics of sex, especially around what is considered normal and abnormal. Yet there are emerging models of sexual health from family social science, child development, and sexology.[4]

As a result, Carnes utilized the teachings of the twelve-step model of Sexaholics Anonymous (SA) and incorporated them into what he calls the twelve dimensions of sexual healthiness.

---

[2] https://www.cdc.gov/sexualhealth.

[3] Stephen Russell, Allen Mallory, Meg Bishop, and Armin Dorri, "Innovation and Integration of Sexuality in Family Life Education," *Family Relations 69*, no. 3 (2020): 595, Accessed October 31, 2023, https://doi.org/10.1111/fare.12462.

[4] Patrick Carnes, PhD, *The 90-Day Prep*.

Below are the twelve dimensions of healthy sexuality:

1. Nurturing
2. Sensuality
3. Self-image
4. Self-definition
5. Comfort
6. Knowledge
7. Relationship
8. Partnership
9. Nongenital sex
10. Genital sex
11. Spirituality
12. Passion

To better understand what each dimension is and how to develop them, I have provided a brief outline of each and how it relates to the twelve-step teachings:

Dimension 1. Nurturing.
Nurturing is the capacity to receive care from others and provide care for oneself. It is important to seek models of nurturing and note how they apply to your sexuality. Plan specific ways to nurture yourself and others—generally, practice acceptance and self-care.

- Care for self and others.
- Accept help.
- If you have a problem, admit you may need help; you cannot fix it on your own.
- Without the foundation of nurturing, healthy sexuality is absent.

This is a first-step principle that asks us to let others care for us and to learn to take care of ourselves. It means giving up control, letting go, and trusting others.

Dimension 2. Sensuality.

Sensuality is the mindfulness of physical senses that create emotional, intellectual, spiritual, and physical presence. Staying focused on the present and being aware of our senses help us increase our sensuality awareness.

It is important to plan concrete and specific ways to notice what your senses are telling you. Integrate your sense awareness into your healthy sexual development.

This is a second-step principle reminding us to seek a "power" higher than ourselves to help us trust that there are larger forces (spiritual) at work in our lives. If we are present in our lives, a sense of wonder will emerge in pursuing our sensuality. Being present allows us to experience what God has designed.

Dimension 3. Self-image.

Self-image is about creating a positive self-perception that includes embracing our sexual self. If self-image is unhealthy, we will need to construct new sexual affirmations about who we are and what we are. From a Christian perspective, Genesis 1:27 NIV tells us, "So God created mankind in his own image, in the image of God he created them; male and female he created them."

We are created for abundant living, fruitfulness, growth, and procreation, as well as for structure and organization. These are all part of God's plan for us. In his image, we are to be great stewards of society and provide care for his created world.

The third step requires faith in ourselves and the belief that a "higher power" (God) made us lovable and sexual.

Dimension 4. Self-definition.

Self-definition is having a clear knowledge of ourselves, both positive and negative, and the ability to express boundaries and needs based on this knowledge. Self-definition is created by knowing who we are and what we are, although not just limited to being a sexual person; it also encompasses the question, "Who am I?"

Self-definition includes all of our character attributes, conscious and unconscious, and mental and physical aspects of our entire being.

Sexually speaking, it is about clarifying sexual priorities and setting boundaries so you can be safe and sexual in healthy ways. It requires you to cultivate discernment through daily meditation, reading, and sensual attunement—all designed to help us stay confidently grounded.

The fourth step asks us to take a "fearless" inventory of who we are, demanding a more honest expression of our innermost needs.

Note: The goal of making a fearless inventory refers to making a list (negative) of the fears, guilt, resentments, hate, and hang-ups we often carry.[5] These are seen as our personal flaws.

Dimension 5. Comfort.

Comfort is the capacity to be at ease about sexual matters with oneself and with others. It is about creating greater comfort about sex by identifying and overcoming negative and dysfunctional family, religious, and cultural messages about sex. It is about confronting issues of sexual preferences and resolving issues created by sexual abuse.

It is essential to acknowledge and accept that we are all wonderfully and fearfully made by God in his image; by seeing ourselves as he sees us, we will begin to accept ourselves just as we are (Psalm 139:14).

The fifth step helps us be fully known by others, including our "dark side." This helps us be comfortable integrating those pieces we used to keep secret and hidden and choosing to carry them no longer.

Dimension 6. Knowledge.

Knowledge is the base of sex in general and about one's unique sexual patterns. It is important to pay attention to the many ways sexual issues enter and affect our day-to-day lives. We are constantly learning about our sexuality as we are beings that go through seasonal changes. Knowledge never needs to stop as we change and mature—we must continue learning, growing, and becoming wiser.

---

[5]   https://www.brcrecovery.com/.

We need to learn to operate based on truth, not popular opinion. We need to develop a plan to learn more about how to understand our healthy sexual selves. The sixth step encourages us to look deeper for "holes" or areas that need work in our lives. Some of our most important lessons come to us here.

Dimension 7. Relationships.

Relationships are the capacity to have intimacy (nonsexual) and friendship with those of the same gender and the opposite gender. Examining our biases about males and females requires comfort, which is about being at ease with both genders. It is essential to learn to separate the erotic from relationships with those of the gender to which you are attracted.

There are four basic relationship types: family, friendships, acquaintances, and romantic, all of which can be considered intimate. An intimate relationship is simply one where trust and vulnerability are experienced within the interdependent relationship. Healthy relationships require honesty, trust, respect, and open communication.

The seventh step allows us to take another leap of faith that these more complex issues will also be overcome. Working them out adds to our spiritual and life experiences.

Dimension 8. Partnership.

Partnership is the ability to maintain an interdependent, equal relationship that is intimate and erotic. It is about exploring how the principles of healthy sexuality can change the rules of abandonment.

It is vital to confront sexual exploitation, abuse, sexualized conflicts, needs, or self-destructive patterns in self or partner/spouse. Learn and practice behaviors that build and enhance your partner/spouse.

A healthy sexual relationship revolves around clear lines of communication; both partners should feel comfortable communicating what they like and dislike regarding sex.

In general, being in a sexual relationship should provide you with a sense of well-being as it meets both your sexual and emotional needs.[6]

The eighth step demands "rigorous" honesty, which becomes central to healthy relationships. This honesty makes all relationships durable and our sexual relationship renewable in its eroticism.

Dimension 9. Nongenital sex.

Nongenital sex is the ability to express erotic desire emotionally and physically without the use of the genitals. It is important to learn more about nongenital touch and planning time to enjoy its pleasures.

Practice includes communicating needs and desires to express what feels good. It is important to reduce the focus on orgasm and, instead, increase emphasis on the whole process of sex. Use touch to acclimatize yourself to more fearful levels of sexual contact gradually.

The ninth step is the action step, which requires us to do what we can to keep our marriages in order. That means using all means that we can and make amends for those areas in which we have not done enough. It also means that we can make up for it when we stop over important parts like nongenital expression.

Dimension 10. Genital sex.

Genital sex is the ability to express erotic feelings with the use of the genitals freely. Identify and work through problems of control and power in sex. Confront impotence and preorgasmic conditions. Review resources on sexual information and techniques. Choose some new sexual techniques and make a plan for experimenting with them.

The tenth step builds on the principles of the previous nine and asks that these principles be practiced in our lives. Few activities demand the integration of these principles more than the use of the genitals.

---

[6] "Guide to Sexual Health: Definition, Importance, and Improving," https://www.pandiahealth.com/resources/guide-to-sexual-health/.

Dimension 11. Spirituality.

Spirituality is the ability to connect sexual desire and expression to the value and meaning of one's life. Seek out models for creating and communicating meaning in sex. Acknowledge the link between sexuality and spirituality.

Biblically speaking, "before the fall—before sin—sex was part of God's created order. It was good—VERY GOOD—and was engaged in freely, without inhibition of any kind by the man and the woman."[7]

Although "the Bible says that sex was affected by the fall, it remains something to be celebrated and protected throughout the entire canon of Scripture."[8]

It may be necessary to examine your sexual history (with a licensed therapist) to determine where you find meaning in sex if you have some concerns. This dimension encourages us to learn to share meaning concurrently and consistently with our partner/spouse.

The eleventh step encourages us to constantly improve our spiritual consciousness. In that way, we remember our connectedness and purpose. Above all, spirituality is about a growing personal, loving relationship with God. Our sexuality needs to be about an intimate, loving, committed relationship (marriage) with our spouse, with God at the center.

Dimension 12. Passion.

Passion is the capacity to express deeply held feelings of desire and meaning about one's self, relationships, and intimate experiences.

Passion is an essential element in building a successful marriage. It is critical to achieving emotional and physical intimacy with your spouse.

Passion is the glue that holds a couple together and keeps the spark alive even during tough times. A passion-fuelled marriage is characterized by a deep sense of connection, intellectual and emo-

---

[7] "5 Surprising Things That the Bible Says about Sex," The Gospel Coalition-Canada, https://ca.thegospelcoalition.org/columns/ad-fontes/5-surprising-things-that-the-bible-says-about-sex/.

[8] Ibid.

tional fulfillment, and maintaining physical attraction toward each other. Without passion, a marriage can quickly lose its depth, reducing it to nothing more than a platonic relationship.

Sadly, many people base passion solely on physical attraction, and physical attraction fades or is lost when our bodies age. Passion has to be more than physical attraction; it must also involve emotional connection and intellectual stimulation.

When spouses share common interests and engage in activities they enjoy, it creates a sense of excitement and enthusiasm that fuels their passion for each other. This shared passion can help strengthen the bond between spouses, naturally creating a deeper level of satisfaction and intimacy.

As we develop and mature, we must learn to develop a passion for stating to our spouse how we have changed due to this process. Share our "conversion"—our new healthy sexual beliefs, values, and ways of living can actively participate in the world around us.

The twelfth step asks that we bear witness to our experience with others. Given the centrality of having the gift of sex in our lives, we can experience healthy sexuality.

Note: The twelve dimensions are more than a series of exercises. They provide basic principles of living. Most of us find opportunities daily to apply one or more of the dimensions to some challenge in our lives. Over time, the spiritual principles in the dimensions become integrated into our thoughts, feelings, and behavior. We find that we are working on the dimensions and living them.

Section 5
Parental Resources

You have all the tools and resources you need.
What you do with them is up to you.
—Cherie Carter-Scott

Parental downloading

Estimated time left: 30 minutes and 1 second
C: reader//87953:downloading_parental_resources

Resource
Common Sexual Terms and Definitions

Listening and understanding your child is key in helping them to open up and talk to you as parents. It is acknowledged that you may have spoken to your child about alcohol, drugs, gaming, or the use of social media. Still, now is the time to talk openly with them about sex (age-appropriate).

In beginning this journey with them, parents need to be up-to-date with current sexual terms and definitions. Kids today have developed unique sexual vocabularies of their own. It is important to know this is not static but a dynamic journey.

To help parents understand sexual vocabulary in today's culture, I have provided a brief list of common sexual terms and their definitions. Hence, you know what they are talking about.

As a parent and grandfather myself, I too have had to keep myself updated by keeping in touch with awareness and understanding of sexual terms, phrases, and *slang* terms being used by the younger generation. We, as parents and grandparents, need to constantly "download" our awareness of what children are being exposed to on the Internet.

Although awkward as it may be, parents have a responsibility to help keep their children safe. Parents must have ongoing conversations with their children about what they will encounter online. It is vital to help guide and support them in keeping the communication relationship open. If parents learn to value the hard work involved, it will go a long way in strengthening the parent-child relationship.

As a parent today, it is encouraged to have ongoing, age-appropriate conversations about *sexual* subject matters as your child grows. This includes explaining what sex is, what consent means, discussing how to spot online predators, as well as everything else sexually. Remember, if you do not, others will, and there may be no chance to teach them what healthy sexuality means.

Lastly, it is important to remember, never shame your child for asking questions—as their parent or guardian, you are an irreplaceable resource for them as they grow and learn.[1]

Parental warning: Explicit sexual words.

For your review, below are common sexual words and phrases, along with their current definitions:

Accountant.

Code word for being a sex worker or involved in sex work. Originating on TikTok as a way to skirt guidelines and censorship. It also is purposed because people do not ask follow-up questions when you say you have a steady, tedious job like an accountant.[2]

Asexual.

A person who does not experience sexual attraction.

Autosexual.

Being attracted to or aroused by yourself.

Bareback.

When you have sex without using protection, like condoms.

---

[1]   https://www.bark.us/blog/sexual-slang/.
[2]   Ibid.

BDSM.

An umbrella term for sexual interests, including bondage, domination, submission/sadism, and masochism.

Bigender.

A person who identifies with both female and male genders. A bigender person may express two genders simultaneously or fluctuate between two genders. Bigender is a gender identity that may or may not inform a person's sexual orientation or sexual preferences.[3]

Bisexual.

A person who is sexually attracted to both men and women.

Cowgirl.

When a person situates themself so they're sitting on top of their partner, legs at the sides of their hips, moving up and down, side to side, around, and more on their partner's penis, sex toy, hand, etc.

Clapping cheeks.

Having sex.

Cruising.

This refers to walking or driving about a locality in search of a sex partner, usually of the anonymous, casual, one-time variety. The term is also used when technology is used to find casual sex, such as using an Internet site or cell or phone service.

---

[3] "What Is Content Filtering? Definition and Types of Content Filters," https:// www.fortinet.com/kr/resources/cyberglossary/content-filtering.

DFT (down with f——k).

Willing to have sex.

Dry humping.

Also known as outercourse, frottage, or dry sex, dry humping is a nonpenetrative sexual activity in which a person grinds against another person or object to elicit pleasure.

Edging.

A technique where you get as close to orgasm as possible or delay your orgasm for as long as possible to ultimately reach a stronger, more powerful orgasm once you release it.

Erectile dysfunction (ED).

A condition in which a male has difficulty getting or maintaining an erection. Erectile dysfunction can result from a physical condition (like bad circulation or low blood pressure) or a psychological condition (like high amounts of stress or low self-confidence) or the result of chronic pornography use.

Erogenous zones.

Erogenous zones are areas of the human body that are especially sensitive. During sexual foreplay, stimulating these areas can encourage relaxation, promote blood flow, build arousal, enhance sexual pleasure, and help you or your partner achieve orgasm. Common erogenous zones include the armpits, lower abdomen, mouth, neck, breasts, buttocks, shoulders, lower back, and genitals.[4]

---

[4] "These Are the Erogenous Zones You Need to Know About," Love My Senses, https://lovemysenses.com/en/2022/05/erogenous-zones-you-need-to-know-about/.

Euphoric recall.

Euphoric recall is when a person remembers the positive sexual experiences associated with their unhealthy sexual behavior rather than the negative consequences it has caused.

Exhibitionism.

A person who gains sexual gratification from the indecent exposure of one's genitals to the public.

Fetish.

This is a form of sexual desire in which gratification is linked to an abnormal degree to a particular object, item of clothing, or part of the body, etc.[5]

Fingering.

Fingering is a sexual technique that involves manual stimulation of the clitoris, vagina, or G-spot during masturbation, foreplay, or penetrative sex. You can perform fingering solo or with a partner of any gender identity or sexual orientation.[6]

Flirting.

This is an expression of sexuality and a common form of social interaction whereby one person implicitly indicates a romantic or sexual interest toward another. However, flirting undertaken for amusement, with no intention of developing any further relationship, poses ethical dilemmas and sometimes faces disapproval from others, either because it can be misinterpreted as more severe or it may be viewed as

---

[5] Crossdressing as Fetish Archives—Living with Crossdressing, https://livingwithcrossdressing.com/tag/crossdressing-as-fetish/.

[6] "The Ultimate Guide to Masturbation: How Do I Finger Myself?" https://thoughtnova.com/ultimate-guide-to-masturbation-how-do-i-finger-myself.

"cheating" if the person flirting is already in a romantic relationship with someone else or if the person to whom flirting is directed is in an exclusive or a serious relationship.

Fondle (sexual).

To touch another person/animal sexually.

Foreplay.

Foreplay is any sexual activity that comes before intercourse. The purpose of foreplay is typically to pave the way for sex. Still, good foreplay can be enjoyable enough to be the main event. Foreplay can involve making out, fingering, dry humping, and nipple stimulation.

Friends with benefits (FWB).

Friends who have a sexual relationship without any commitment.

Frotteurism.

The practice of achieving sexual stimulation or orgasm by touching or rubbing against a person without the person's consent.

GNOC.

Short for "get naked on camera." (Used online or in text messages.)[7]

---

[7]   https://www.bark.us/blog/sexual-slang/.

Gender dysphoria.

This is the discomfort or distress that might occur in people whose gender identity differs from their sex assigned at birth or sex-related physical characteristics.[8]

Gender-nonconforming.

An umbrella term that describes anyone whose gender expression or identity does not align with traditional societal expectations.[9] Gender-nonconforming is a gender identity that may or may not inform a person's sexual orientation or preferences.

Gender fluid.

A person who is gender fluid may always feel like a mix of the two traditional genders but may feel more boy some days and girl other days.[10] Being gender fluid has nothing to do with which set of genitalia one has or one's sexual orientation.

Genderqueer.

An umbrella term for a person who doesn't identify with a single gender identity. This term overlaps with nonbinary and can also describe anyone who is not cisgender.[11] Genderqueer is a gender identity that may or may not inform a person's sexual orientation or sexual preferences.

---

[8] "The Ultimate Guide to Masturbation: How Do I Finger Myself?" https://thoughtnova.com/ultimate-guide-to-masturbation-how-do-i-finger-myself.

[9] Ibid.

[10] "Zeitgeist Today," https://www.moondays.com/blog/zeitgeist-today.

[11] "List of 72 Genders and Their Meanings," Public Health, https://www.publichealth.com.ng/list-of-72-genders-and-their-meanings/.

Gender identity.

A person's understanding of their gender may or may not correlate with their assigned gender at birth, gender expression, sexual orientation, sexual attraction, or the particular gender roles or traditional gender binary of their society.[12] Many gender variants make up the gender spectrum, such as male, female, agender, bigender, transgender, femme, intersex, and gender fluid.

Gender expression.

How a person presents their gender to those around them. Gender expression consists of many different elements, including clothing, grooming, mannerisms, behavior, and interests.[13] Gender expression is a part of gender identity.[14]. It may or may not inform a person's sexual orientation or preferences.

GYAT.

A shortened term for "god———n." Used to express approval or excitement. Often, it is used in response to seeing a girl that one finds attractive (particularly with a curvy body).[15]

Heteronormativity.

Heteronormativity is the belief that heterosexuality is the only natural expression of sexuality.[16]

---

[12] "Karta, Halmstad Köp Nu Betala Sen," Tavlero.se, https://enklapengargotg.netlify.app/60022/47593.html.

[13] "Zeitgeist Today," https://www.moondays.com/blog/zeitgeist-today.

[14] "Wellness," https://wellness.healthysteps4u.org/archives/2772.

[15] https://www.bark.us/blog/sexual-slang/.

[16] "On the Margins with Full Equality Still Out of Reach," Officers Pulse, https://officerspulse.com/on-the-margins-with-full-equality-still-out-of-reach/.

Heterosexual.

Sexually attracted to people of the opposite sex.

Homosexual/Gay/Lesbian.

A person sexually attracted to people of their sex.

IWSN.

Short for "I want sex now."

Incest (incestuous relationship).

An overly close relationship that seems improper or inappropriate sexual behavior between family members (e.g., biological, fostered, adopted, blended, or step).

Intersex.

A person born with ambiguously gendered bodies due to chromosome anomalies or ambiguous genitalia. Intersex people often receive a gender assignment at birth through medical intervention, which may or may not correspond to the gender they identify with as they age.[17] Intersexuality is a part of gender identity and may or may not inform a person's sexual orientation or sexual preferences.

Kink.

A nontraditional sexual interest that a person derives arousal or pleasure from but doesn't necessarily need for sexual gratification. Kinky sex refers to sexual activities and preferences that fall outside standard sexual practices, like making out, masturbation, oral sex,

---

[17] "List of 72 Genders and Their Meanings," Public Health, https://www.publichealth.com.ng/list-of-72-genders-and-their-meanings/.

and anal sex—though kinks are widely practiced and increasingly accepted as the social norm. Common types of kinks include bondage, cuckolding (having a sexual relationship with another man's wife), role-playing, voyeurism, and sadomasochism.

Legg booty.

Refers to LGBTQ.[18]

LGBTQIA+?

Is an abbreviation for lesbian, gay, bisexual, transgender, queer or questioning, intersex, asexual ("ace"), and more. These terms describe a person's sexual orientation or gender identity.

Masturbation.

The act of pleasuring yourself for sexual enjoyment. Masturbation can employ several different tools—hands, toys like dildos or vibrators, erotic videos or stories, or even just mental imagery—and can be done solo or with a partner(s) as part of mutual masturbation.

Molest.

To harm a person/animal through sexual contact.

Monogamy.

The practice of engaging in a relationship (sexual or romantic) with only one other person at a time. Monogamy contrasts polyamory, in which a person can simultaneously engage in multiple relationships.

---

[18] https://www.bark.us/blog/sexual-slang/.

Nip nops.

Nipples.[1]

Nonbinary.

A person who doesn't fall under the traditional male-female binary. A nonbinary person may identify as both male and female or neither. Nonbinary is a gender identity that may or may not inform a person's sexual orientation or sexual preferences.

One-night stand.

A single sexual encounter without expecting further relations between the sexual participants. This is regardless of whether either participant initially intended a single meeting to be a one-night stand or whether further relations between the participants subsequently arise.[2]

Oral sex.

When a person uses their mouth to stimulate another's genitals. Oral stimulation can be performed using the tongue, lips, or throat. It can be a form of foreplay before sexual intercourse or as the main event of a sexual experience.[3] Oral sex has three subcategories: cunnilingus (oral sex with a vulva), fellatio (oral sex with a penis, also called a blow job), and analingus (oral sex with an anus, also called a rim job).

Orgy.

Three or more people having sex together or one after the other.

---

[1] https://www.bark.us/blog/sexual-slang/.

[2] "How Much Are You Loved?" CustomerThink, https://customerthink.com/how-much-are-you-loved/.

[3] "Easy Steps to Give Good Oral Sex," IFONNX, https://ifonnx.com/blogs/vibrator-guides/5-easy-steps-to-give-good-oral-sex.

Pansexual.

A person not limited in sexual choice concerning biological sex, gender, or gender identity.

Pegging.

A sex act in which one person has anal sex with another person by penetrating them with a strap-on dildo.[4] Pegging can be done by and to people of any gender or sexual orientation.

Polyamory.

The practice of engaging in multiple relationships (sexual or romantic) at one time; these relationships are called "polyamorous relationships." Polyamory directly contrasts monogamy, in which a person is engaged romantically or sexually in one relationship at one time.

Pornography.

Although subjective to each individual, porn explicitly portrays sexual subject matter for sexual arousal. Pornography may be presented in various media, including books, magazines, postcards, photographs, sculptures, drawings, paintings, animations, sound recordings, films, videos, or video games.

Seggs.

Alternate spelling of "sex."[5]

---

[4]   "Different Ways to Engage in Anal Play," Blush, http://blog.blushnovelties. com/blog/different-ways-to-engage-in-anal-play/.

[5]   https://www.bark.us/blog/sexual-slang/.

Sexual fantasy.

A person with a one-way interest in another sexually (the other person does not know). This occurs through feeling or thought.

Sexual rubber necking.

This is the act of gawking at someone or something of sexual interest repeatedly.

Shipping.

This means creating a romantic pairing between two people not otherwise romantically linked or connected.

Smash.

Means to have casual sex.

Sneaky link.

Term for someone you're hooking up with on the sly.[6]

Spicy eggplant.

Vibrator.[7]

Thirsty.

Desperate for sexual attention; horny.

---

[6] Ibid.
[7] Ibid.

Transsexual (adjective)/*transgender* (noun).

A person whose bodily characteristics have been altered through surgery or hormone treatment to align with their gender identity.

Virtual girl/male friend.

Using any Internet site or app to create a virtual partner for sexual or nonsexual purposes.

Voyeurism.

A person who watches others (unknown to others) for sexual pleasure, arousal, or interest. Someone who gains satisfaction from watching others, especially secretly, other people's bodies, or sexual acts they may be participating in.

Resource
Social Media Apps/ Online Platforms

Most everyone uses social media for a variety of reasons. Social media provides endless possibilities, whether for photo or video sharing, personal or business networking, gaming, dating, gambling, chatting with friends or others worldwide, or keeping up with the latest news or trends.

Because social media platforms change frequently, parents need to learn about the apps their children are using to help keep them safe.

As of the writing of this book, updated in November 2023, several prominent social media platforms were in use. However, the landscape of social media is constantly evolving, and new platforms may have emerged or gained prominence since then. Here are some of the popular social media platforms that were popular at that time:

- BeReal
- Bluesky Social
- Classmates
- CounterSocial
- CutStory
- Discord
- Douyin
- Facebook
- Flickr
- Flixster
- Friendster

- Hootsuite
- Instagram
- Line
- LinkedIn
- Mastodon
- Messenger
- Meetup
- Minds
- Myspace
- Nextdoor
- Pinterest
- Polywork
- Qzone
- Reddit
- Sina Weibo
- Snapchat
- Supernova
- Tagged
- Telegram
- Tencent QC
- TikTok
- Tinder
- Tsocial
- Tumblr
- Twitch
- Twitter
- YouTube
- Yubo
- WeChat
- WhatsApp

Note: The popularity of social media platforms can change rapidly, and new platforms can emerge. To get the most current information on the social media landscape, I recommend checking the latest news and statistics on the Internet or app stores.

Resource
Social Media—Parental Controls

Parental controls for social media are essential tools that can help parents and guardians monitor and limit their children's access to social media platforms. These controls are designed to protect children from inappropriate content, online predators, and excessive screen time.[1]

From a basic understanding, parental control products contain tools to block inappropriate website content. Typically, this is category-based. But most products also include the ability to configure "whitelists" and "blacklists."[2]

Note: Category-based filtering enables organizations to restrict access to specific categories of websites, such as adult gambling, online shopping, or social networking sites. This offers a more dynamic approach to policy implementation and more control over how users access the Internet.[3]

In researching the best of best blocking tools, the information below is provided by *"The Best Parental Control App Service* of 2023."* Please keep in mind the continued growth of social media is ever-changing.

Whitelists are lists of websites that the administrator (e.g., parent) has deemed to be okay—a whitelisted website will not be

---

[1] ChatGPT, prompt "What are some parental controls for social media," October 20, 2023, OpenAI, https://chat.openai.com.

[2] "The Best Parental Control App Services of 2023," https://www.top10.com/parental-control.

[3] "What Is Content Filtering? Definition and Types of Content Filters," https://www.fortinet.com/kr/resources/cyberglossary/content-filtering.

blocked even if it is classified as belonging to a blocked category. Conversely, a blacklisted website will not be allowed to display even when the category is not blocked.[4]

Additionally, most parental control tools have functions that can control or limit the amount of time the child spends using their electronic device.

These functions allow parents to restrict access to the Internet during certain hours of the day. Let's say you want to block specific programs or prevent the Internet from running after 9:00 p.m.— when children should prepare for bed rather than sit at the PC.

Many programs also allow parents to limit the number of hours per day during which the Internet, specific programs, or the computer can be utilized. If the daily hour limit is exceeded, the child will be prevented from being able to access the website in question.[5]

Parents have various options for controlling their children's software and apps. It is vital to choose a software or app that is designed to protect them from age-inappropriate content.

Examples of content types typically blocked include pornography, websites containing violence, and websites promoting the sale of vaping products and alcoholic beverages.

Listed below are some steps and strategies for setting up parental controls for social media:

Start with open communication.

Before implementing strict controls, talk to your children about the reasons behind these measures. Explain the potential risks of social media and the importance of responsible usage.

---

[4] "The Best Parental Control App Services of 2023," https://www.top10.com/parental-control.

[5] Ibid.

Use built-in platform controls.

Many social media platforms offer built-in parental control features. For example, Facebook, Instagram, and TikTok provide options to restrict who can contact your child and who can see their content. You can also set account privacy settings to limit who can follow or interact with them.

Install monitoring apps.

Various third-party apps and software allow parents to monitor their child's social media activity. Note: *See the "Parental Software and Apps" section below for more information.*

Time limits.

Implement screen time limits for social media usage. Both android and iOS devices offer parental control features that allow parents to set daily or weekly time limits for specific apps, including social media.

Filtering and blocking.

Utilize content filtering and blocking features to prevent your child from accessing inappropriate content. These filters can be applied at the router level, on specific devices, or within certain apps.

Location tracking.

Some parental control apps offer GPS tracking, which can help you keep tabs on your child's location when they are using social media.

Educate your child.

Teach your child about online safety, privacy, and the potential consequences of their online actions. Encourage them to report any concerning interactions or messages.

Regularly review and adjust.

As your child grows and gains more responsibility, adjust the parental controls accordingly. Regularly review the settings and discuss any changes with your child.

Lead by example.

Children often learn by observing their parents. Promote responsible and safe social media usage as a good digital role model.

Stay informed.

Parents need to keep up-to-date with the latest trends in social media and online safety. New platforms and challenges emerge; parents must know what their children may encounter online.

Parental controls for social media can vary depending on the platform, the device, and your family's specific needs. Here are some common parental control features and settings you can use on some of the common social media platforms and devices:

Facebook

Privacy settings. Adjust the privacy settings for your child's Facebook account to control who can see their posts, who can send them friend requests, and who can look them up using their email address or phone number.

Messenger Kids. Facebook offers Messenger Kids, a child-friendly messaging app with parental controls that allow you to approve contacts and monitor conversations.

Instagram

Private account. Set your child's Instagram account to private so they have to approve followers.

Restricted accounts. You can restrict specific accounts to limit interactions with them.

Comment controls. Enable comment filters to block or hide offensive comments.

Activity dashboard. Instagram's activity dashboard shows time spent on the platform.

Twitter (now X)

Protected tweets. Make your child's tweets protected so only approved followers can see them.

Muted words and accounts. Use Twitter's (X) mute feature to hide specific words, phrases, or accounts from your child's timeline.

Safety mode. Twitter (X) offers a "safety mode" feature to automatically block accounts that might be harmful.

Snapchat

Privacy settings. Adjust the privacy settings to control who can send your child snaps, view their stories, and see their location.

Snap Map. Turn on Ghost Mode to hide your child's location on the Snap Map.

Memories backup. Limit the ability to back up snaps to memories.

TikTok

Family Pairing. TikTok offers a Family Pairing feature that allows parents to link their TikTok account to their child's and set restrictions on screen time, content, and messaging.

Privacy settings. Adjust the privacy settings, including who can comment, duet, or stitch your child's videos.

YouTube

YouTube Kids. Consider using the YouTube Kids app, which offers a curated and more child-friendly content selection.

Restricted mode. Enable restricted mode on the regular YouTube app to filter out potentially mature content.

Watch and search history. Review and clear watch and search history to limit the recommendations your child receives.

Device-level parental controls

Both android and iOS devices offer built-in parental control features that allow you to set app limits and screen time restrictions. You can use these to limit your child's time on social media apps.

Use third-party parental control apps like Qustodio, Norton Family, or Net Nanny to monitor and control your child's device usage, including social media apps.

Final thoughts: It is essential to explore each platform's specific settings and controls and adjust them according to your child's age, maturity, and family needs.

Additionally, it's crucial to have open communication with your child about these controls to foster responsible online behavior.

Remember that while parental controls can provide a safety net, open communication and education are crucial to helping your child develop responsible online behavior. It's essential to strike a balance between protecting them and allowing them to learn how to navigate the online world responsibly.[6]

Parental Software Programs

1. Aura

---

[6] "Unveiling the Dark Web: A Comprehensive Guide," https://marketsplash. com/dark-web/.

     https://buy.aura.com

2. Bark
   https://www.bark.us

3. Boomerang
   https://useboomerang.com

4. Canopy
   https://www.canopy.us

5. Eyezy
   https://www.eyezy.com

6. Familykeeper
   https://www.familykeeper.reasonlab.com

7. FamilyTime
   https://www.familytime.io

8. Kidslox
   https://www.kidslox.com

9. Microsoft Family Safety
   htpps://www.microsoft.com/en-us/microsoft-365/family-safety

10. Mobicip
    https://www.mobicip.com

11. mSpy
    https://mspy.net

12. Net Nanny
    https://www.netnanny.com

13. Norton Family
    https://www.norton.com

14. Qustodio
    https://www.qustodio.com

Note: The software and apps listed above were available during print. Most, if not all, provide real-time alerts while others may provide detailed reports on your child's online behavior.

Resource
Internet (Pornography) Accountability Software

Internet accountability software is designed to prevent and hold accountable access to pornography websites, adult entertainment, objectionable content, and any other content deemed to be inappropriate by the licensee.

Generally speaking, these programs can be installed on many devices, such as smartphones, tablets, and desktop PCs. Some people install Internet accountability software on their own devices to keep themselves accountable to other people. Still, other people install accountability software on their children's devices and computers to keep their children accountable.

Internet filters can be helpful, but they have their limitations. It is important to remember that regardless of which accountability program you choose, it will not "cure" your child from the lure of temptation.

Internet Accountability Software Programs

1. Accountable2You
   https://www.accountable2you.com
2. Bark
   https://www.bark.us
3. Canopy
   https://www.canopy.us

4. Covenant Eyes
    htpps://www.covenanteyes.com
5. EverAccountable
    https://www.everyaccountable.com
6. Freedom
    https://www.freedom.to
7. Lion Accountability Browser
    https://www.accountability.software
8. X3Watch
    https://www.z3watch.com

Author's Reflection

Parenting today is a complex and multifaceted endeavor, shaped by various factors, including societal changes, technological advancements, and the overall pressures parents have.

Today's parents have to navigate the digital landscape, where technology is an integral part of their children's lives. They face the challenge of balancing screen time, ensuring online safety, and promoting healthy technology usage.

Adding possible further challenges, today's families come in diverse forms, including single-parent families, blended families, same-sex parent families, and more. This diversity has led to a shift in traditional family roles and dynamics, impacting how parents approach their responsibilities.

Many parents are having to juggle the demands of work and family life. Achieving a balance that allows for quality time with children while meeting career obligations is an ongoing challenge.

Furthermore, there is a growing recognition of the importance of mental health in children and parents. The stigma around mental health issues is decreasing, allowing families to seek support and resources more openly. Parental well-being and self-care are receiving increased attention. Parents are encouraged to prioritize their physical and emotional health to be more effective caregivers.

Challenges such as bullying, peer pressure, and the impact of social media on children's self-esteem are topics that parents must address.

Without question, parenting today is a dynamic and ever-evolving process. Parents must adapt to the changing landscape while maintaining a focus on their children's well-being, values, and development. The role of a parent remains one of the most significant and rewarding responsibilities, and it requires constant learning and adaptation to provide the best possible upbringing for the next generation.

When I embarked on writing this book, I knew that parenting was a subject close to my heart. Still, I quickly realized that delving into it on a deeper level was both humbling and enlightening. Parenting is not merely about offering advice or sharing expert opinions. It's a profoundly personal journey, and the experience of writing about it has deepened my appreciation for the diversity of approaches and challenges we, as parents, face.

I hope that this book will serve as a source of insight, understanding, inspiration, guidance, and affirmation for all those who embark on the adventure of parenting and that it will remind us that, in the end, it's the journey itself that holds the most profound lessons and rewards.

Parental download complete

Estimated time left: 0 hours and 0 seconds
C: reader//87953:downloading_complete

About the Author

 John Sternfels is a licensed professional counselor and an American author of three books: *A Partner's Guide To Truth & Healing* (Amazon's number 1 best-selling book in the mental health category October 2021) and, new for 2024, *Behind the Smile* and *DOWNLOAD for Parents*. John earned his master's degree in counseling psychology from Liberty University. He is the owner and clinical director of NorthPoint Professional Counseling, located in Novi, Michigan. John is a national certified counselor (NCC) and holds advanced training and certifications as a certified sexual addiction therapist (CSAT), certified multiple addiction therapist (CMAT), certified clinical partner specialist (CCPS), and certified clinical sexual addiction specialist (C-SASI) and is trained in Gottman marriage therapy and EMDR.

Throughout the year, John facilitates numerous local and online workshops, seminars, and support groups for both men and women—all designed to improve relational healing, intimacy, and healthiness.

John is married to his wife, Kathy, and they are grandparents to five wonderful grandchildren.